FAMILY PORTRAITS
IN
CHANGING TIMES

HELEN NESTOR

Foreword by Judith Stacey, Ph. D.

NEWSAGE PRESS

FAMILY PORTRAITS IN CHANGING TIMES

Address inquiries to NewSage Press, P.O. Box 607, Troutdale, Oregon 97060-0607

First Edition 1992

Printed in Hong Kong through Print Vision, Portland, Oregon

ISBN 0-939165-16-3 (Clothbound)

ISBN 0-939165-15-5 (Softcover)

Library of Congress
Cataloging-in-Publication Data

Nestor, Helen.

    Family portraits in changing times / by Helen Nestor: foreword by Judith Stacey.

    p. cm.

    Summary: First person profiles of thirty-three nontraditional contemporary American families.

    ISBN 0-939165-16-3 : $39.95.
    ISBN 0-939165-15-5 (pbk.): $22.95

    1. Family—United States. 2. Family—United States—Pictorial works. 3. Life style—United States. 4. Life style—United States—Pictorial works. [1.Family—Personal narratives.]

    I. Title

HQ536.N47 1992

306.85'0973—dc20   92-5341

Acknowledgments

I am immensely grateful to all of the families who agreed to participate in this project, to open their lives to my view of them and to my camera, to write with honesty about their feelings and personal experience of "family" and to make themselves vulnerable to public scrutiny. Many could not be included because of space limitations—for them a special thanks. Heartfelt thanks are also due to the many friends and acquaintances who referred me to families whom they knew personally, and to their relatives and associates.

To the MacDowell Colony, the Ragdale Foundation, the Virginia Center for the Creative Arts, and the Djerassi Foundation, my deep appreciation for fellowships to work in an atmosphere of encouragement and support and uninterrupted time and space where the focus was to provide an environment for doing one's best work. These residential fellowships also provided me with an opportunity to photograph families in other parts of the country.

There are individuals without whom *Family Portraits in Changing Times* could never have occurred. Sheila Ballantyne encouraged and urged me on from the start, offering her faith in the project and her keen advice, and reassuring me at every turn. Thanks are also due to my assistants, Becky Dolhinow, Ann Colt, Julie Christiansen, Cory O'Hama, and Kelsey Lowitz, who worked with me during the final year of photographing, sensitively "fading into the woodwork" so as not to interfere with the special relationship that takes place between photographer and subject. When I saw the NewSage Press book, *A Portrait of American Mothers and Daughters*, I knew that this was the publisher I wanted for my book. My publisher and editor, Maureen R. Michelson, has not disappointed me. With her vision of the final work, she has patiently and carefully guided me to its fruition with caring advice and fine tuning, despite my frequent resistance along the way. And finally, my most special thanks to my husband, Byron Nestor, who supported my involvement with the project for more than a decade, endlessly looking at proof sheets and intuitively knowing and guiding me to the frame that most closely reflected my gut feelings at the moment of exposure, and, as though that weren't enough, learned to cook to conserve my enegy.

For my granddaughters, Ruth, Leah, and Sarah.

Contents

When Helen Nestor first invited me to write a foreword to this extraordinary book, I resisted. I had recently written a book, *Brave New Families: Stories of Upheaval in Late Twentieth-Century America*, saying about as much as I had ever hoped to say about the character and meaning of recent changes in American family life. Far more inhibiting, however, was the power and poignancy I found in the photographic and autobiographical documents of contemporary family diversity that this exquisite book contains. Which "thousand words" could an academic analyst of family transformation possibly offer to equal these riveting photographs and personal statements? None, I argued, that would do more to augment than to diminish their cumulative impact.

Readers will need little encouragement from me to proceed directly to the introduction and the mesmerizing portrait of Helen Nestor's own paternal family, which, she tells us, first inspired her passion for family photography. Photographed in their San Francisco home in 1906, the Dinkelspiel portrait—an engrossing image of a late Victorian family—must have been composed on the historical eve of the cataclysmic earthquake whose reverberations still haunt that region of the country.

A seismic shift of equal magnitude and even more irrevocable significance is the subject of *Family Portraits in Changing Times*. Indeed, this social trembler, which I call the "postmodern family revolution," defeated the original plans that Helen Nestor conceived for this project. Eleven years after she had begun her visual ethnographic study of changing family life in 1977 with a photographic exhibit of forty "nontraditional" families, she set out to revisit and record their evolution. The quixotic nature of this quest became readily apparent. Of the forty original families first photographed in the 1970s, only eleven were available to be rephotographed. Individual families, like the individual humans who compose them, are always in flux. Not even many traditional families in less turbulent periods would have stood still long enough over eleven years to pose for their second portraits. But these particular eleven years, and the two decades that preceded them, comprise a momentous period in American family history. Not only have individual families changed unrecognizably, but economic and social upheavals have thrown the very definition of what constitutes a family into a state of extended, animated social contest. Proponents of "domestic partners" and "family diversity" legislation compete with "prolife" and "profamily" activists to oversee public representations of, and access to, resources for American families because the majority of ordinary Americans have forfeited and/or abandoned what was taken for granted for so long—a shared notion of what constitutes an ordinary American family.

The ordinary American family for more than a century prior to this tumult—one which Helen Nestor, like most Americans today, terms the *traditional* family—consisted of a man and woman rearing their 2.3 birth children. I would restrict this definition somewhat further and revise its moniker. Both Helen Nestor in the 1920s and I in the 1940s grew up in a society whose "ordinary" family housed a male breadwinner, a female homemaker and their 2.3 biological offspring. Three-fifths of American households still contained this sort of ordinary family in 1950, but fewer than 10 percent do so today. That is why these now appear *traditional* to us, even though, in the long view of Western history, the breadwinner-homemaker nuclear household was a decidedly *modern innovation*. In the premodern period, home and work sites were integrated and the labor of women was as visible and crucial to family survival as was the labor of men.

In any case, this endangered species of human kin arrangements serves as the phantom foil for this book's mission, as it did for my own ethnographic study of family change, and as it does, I believe, for the American political unconscious. The dizzying rapidity with which such modern nuclear families have been supplanted by the diverse array of family forms portrayed in *Family Portraits in Changing Times*—blended families, matrilineal families, adoptive families, gay families, single-father families, female breadwinner-homemaker father families, physically disabled adoptive-parent families, cohabiting parent families, in vitro-generated families, and many more— unsettles many of us and nourishes prophets of doom. Family change has become a prism, and too often a scapegoat, for viewing threatening dislocations in our economic and social order. Unconstructive nostalgia for the idealized ordinary families of yesteryear breeds intolerance for the kind of family and social diversity that is the new ordinary condition of late twentieth century life. The poet Auden once cautioned that "we must learn to love one another or die." Perhaps we need not learn to love one another's families or die, but we certainly need to learn to live with them more hospitably.

Family Portraits in Changing Times is the ideal antidote to retro-traditional family sentiments as well as an intensive tutorial in the family tolerance curriculum we sorely need. Helen Nestor and her family subjects do not flinch from recording many of the personal costs of old and new family traumas. Words and images of family members suffering from neglect, abuse, AIDS, unemployment, divorce, teen pregnancy, physical and mental disabilities, racist stigmata, infertility, and other traumas document family anguish and struggle. But this book is not a pictorial sermon about family decay. Instead, Helen Nestor has turned her profoundly respectful photographic gifts to a more illuminating task. Despite the staggering level of challenges families now confront and the miserly level of public support they receive, legions of intentional and unwitting pioneers of a postmodern family revolution have expended their creative, resilient, often inspirational energies to fashion from old and new kinship resources a kaleidoscopic array of "brave new families." This book's artful, empathic, photographic-essay collage celebrates their quiet heroism. I am confident that readers will join me in celebrating the quiet heroism of Helen Nestor, who triumphed over her own physical adversities to bless the many ever-changing families who will find solace, insight, and affirmation in *Family Portraits in Changing Times*.

Judith Stacey, Ph.D.

I can't recall a time when I wasn't thinking about making my own family. As a young child in the 1920s, I took for granted that when I grew up I would marry, stay home, and have children like my mom. I fondly remember the endless and elaborate "weddings" my older sister, Katy, and I staged with our large family of dolls in the fragrant garden patio of our neighbor's home. My early teens coincided with the Depression. My father lost his job. The family car was repossessed. We children were advised not to open the door to bill collectors, and I decided that I needed to make a career—just in case my dream of marriage and children didn't work out. Times were changing. I decided to make a career in the public health field, hoping I might meet a doctor to marry. I had rejected the possibility of *being* a doctor since I had passively accepted my feminine fate.

As it happened, my sister married immediately upon graduation from college. Following her example, I did the same—yes, to a doctor. But unlike my mother, I had a family and a career. What had begun as a desire to document the fast disappearing innocence of my own children in the late 1950s, had developed into a passion for making photographs and my work as a professional photographer. The 1950s were a momentous time in the history of photography, and I was fortunate to be able to study with Ansel Adams, Minor White, and Morley Baer, as well as to know personally Dorothea Lange, who became my mentor.

A few months before my mother died in 1966, she went through hundreds of family photographs stored in an old teak chest and created a new album she titled "Five Generations." It traced the family history back to my great-grandparents who immigrated to San Francisco from Germany in the 1850s. She wanted her grandchildren—my children—to know who they were. With white ink on the black album pages, in her careful handwriting, my mother identified each individual and the years of their birth and death. She must have gotten the information partly from memory, partly from visits to family plots in the cemetery, and partly from the detailed family trees my Aunt Alice made for her grandnieces and grandnephews.

Over the years I browsed through this special book, lingering over a 1906 portrait of my father's family in the living room of their Jackson Street home in San Francisco. The photographer is unknown, but whether or not she or he was personally acquainted with them, the members of my family are accurately revealed as the individuals I came to know more than twenty years later. I loved the Victorian living room, which so clearly delineated their time. I became so absorbed with the picture that I made a larger print, and for years I have never tired of looking at it, studying it, wondering about the qualities that make this photograph such a strong work. Intimations of the way family members' lives would play themselves out later are in the photograph, revealed in subtle ways by their body and facial expressions, the objects they chose to hold in their hands, and the way they positioned themselves in relation to one another.

Inspired by this early photograph of my father's family, I decided to photograph families of my time. Thinking about the changes that were taking place in my own family and in friends' families, I was aware of great variations from the accepted image of the traditional family. Two of my three children, who were in their 20s at the time, were living in communal families. More of my friends were divorced than not. Few were grandparents. My son doubted that he would want to have children before he was 40. Few of my friends' children were married. A longtime friend was soon to become a grandmother. Her son, the father, was not married. The times were changing.

The variety of new family constellations and new kinds of relationships appearing in the 1970s seemed unending. From all quarters questions were being raised about the past, present, and future of the family. None of the studies, conferences, books, or reports satisfied my curiosity. I decided to take a look for myself, to photograph the new kinds of families I saw around me.

Helen Nestor's paternal family, the Dinkelspiels, in their Victorian living room in 1906.

I chose to photograph nontraditional families which, for my project, I defined as any family other than a man and woman who are married and rearing their two and one-third biological birth children, with the father as the breadwinner and the mother as the homemaker. Nontraditional families also included those families who were breaking away from the norm of cultural, racial, and economic similarities. I decided to limit the families to those who were rearing children, which meant excluding a friend who considered her beloved dog as family. I wanted to place the families as strongly in their era and relating to me, the photographer, as had that unknown photographer who photographed my family seventy years earlier. I wanted to explore not only the fabric of the families, but also the complicated relationships that operate within them. The resulting series of nontraditional family portraits of the 1970s was shown in gallery exhibitions nationally and in magazines heralding the "changing family."

For eleven years my photographs were stored in archival boxes. In 1988 I decided to rephotograph the original forty families to explore how they had fared in the intervening years. There had been tremendous changes during the past decade. In 1970 the traditional American family unit was found in about 40 percent of U.S. households. By 1990 less than 15 percent of American families were comprised of a breadwinner father, homemaker mother, and their two children.

As I began my search for the original forty families, some of whom I had not contacted in ten years, it soon became apparent that many of the families had disintegrated, divorced, broken up, regrouped, moved to distant places, or disappeared. I realized it would be impossible to rephotograph many of them. There had been painful breakups: some family members wanted nothing to do with the others and did not want to be photographed with them. New partners did not want to participate in a project involving their partner's former mate.

Children had grown and moved from the family home and could not or would not manage a time to regroup for a family sitting. Some of the grown children did not want to be placed in the public eye via a book. In one case, as I was photographing an interracial family, a grown son, now a father himself, stepped out of the frame. He didn't want to be in the picture, saying, "It is like our lives are out there on view again." He didn't want to be included in a series of photographs of what he called "freaks." A painful and tearful family confrontation ensued, and my assistant and I packed up our equipment and departed. In another family, a college professor who had chosen to become a mother in 1974, did not want her secret—that she had not been married to her daughter's father—divulged to the conservative academic community in which she found herself ten years later. In two cases adopted children had been removed by the authorities from the single adults who had adopted them. Three divorced women who had been sharing a house with their three daughters did not wish to be rephotographed. All had remarried and it had not been a time they wanted to remember.

I gradually came to realize that what I regarded as the nontraditional family in the 1980s, simply because of its composition, had been supplemented by change not only in composition, but also in ways of functioning and role definition within the family. Judith Stacey, a professor of sociology, calls this the "postmodern family." In her book, *Brave New Families*, Stacey writes, "No longer is there a single, culturally dominant family pattern to which the majority of Americans conform and most of the rest of us aspire. Instead, Americans today have crafted a multiplicity of family and household arrangements that we inhabit uneasily and reconstitute frequently in response to changing personal and occupational circumstances."

Of the forty original families I photographed, only nine are included in *Family Portraits in Changing Times*. To supplement the original group with additional families, I sought various ways families are being "remade." As I travelled to photograph families, I found that the remaking and redefining of the traditional family is nationwide. I loved meeting and becoming acquainted with the families in the process of photographing, having the opportunity to ask what may have seemed impertinent questions in a more social setting. My intentions remained the same as in the original series: to reveal as honestly as I was able the way they live together, interactions within the family, and suggestions of the home environment. I asked each family to present themselves in a place and manner that most clearly fit their self-image and felt most comfortable to them. I did not direct how they should arrange themselves for the photograph. Often I felt an urge to continue the relationship after the photo session and felt sorrow at parting, knowing I would not see them again.

Several family members told me that writing about family was much more difficult and emotionally involving than they had anticipated. While a few families presented me with family statements when I arrived to photograph, others, in spite of their best intentions, procrastinated for months before writing down their experience of family. In some cases, people were surprised to find out how rewarding the task turned out to be, while others refused to write. The families first photographed in the 1970s had not been asked to write about their fami-

lies, and when I contacted them ten years later, some did not want to participate. I had a hard time letting go of some of my favorite photographs.

The written comments, like the photographs, record only a moment in time. I
learned of important changes in some families and their thinking about them
only a few months after they had been photographed and written their statements. I realized families are always changing and what family members wrote
about their feelings and observations of family may represent only a particular
moment in time, just as my photographs represent only a particular moment on
a particular day in their lives.

I photographed in the 1970s using crutches, and in the late 1980s and early
1990s I used a combination of crutches and a three-wheeled motorized scooter.
A part of me has always refused to accept that I could not continue my life as I
had before I had polio in 1951, just before the Salk vaccine was discovered. As a
result of the late effects of poliomyelitis, I am losing muscle strength that I had
regained the year after the original attack and am now using a wheelchair most
of the time. I was concerned that my subjects would feel uncomfortable with
my inability to be in physical charge of the photographic session and would
want to help me and get caught up in that process rather than simply assuming
their roles as subjects and members of the families. Although this did occur to
some extent, I felt that it was outweighed by my own vulnerability, which put
them at ease in a situation where they, as the subjects, were feeling especially
vulnerable. Photographing Denise and Neil Jacobson, who are both in wheelchairs, and their son, David, proved to be an hilarious occasion. Imagine three
adults in wheelchairs, 2-year-old David, the only able-bodied person present,
and me trying to capture a still moment with Denise and Neil, who have difficulty controlling their reflexive movements.

During the final year of photographing I was struggling to complete the work
while my hands and arms were still able to efficiently operate the camera and
while I was still able to climb the stairs to my subjects' homes. I had been committed to this project for fourteen years and passionately wanted to bring it to
the conclusion I had dreamed of. Years ago Dorothea Lange, who had polio as
child, told me I must have an assistant. I resisted this good advice from
Dorothea, whom I idolized. But having an assistant to carry my equipment,
help with the stairs, and move my tripod—the idea of which I'd rejected in the
past as interfering with the intimate relationship between me and the families—was a tremendous help.

I began this project with few preconceptions, only my awareness of what a
nuclear family had been in the past and curiosity about what family patterns are
now evolving. I wanted to document as many different family situations as I
could find. I now see "family" as any of a multitude of possibilities. My hope is
that *Family Portraits in Changing Times* will create a greater awareness, as well
as understanding and acceptance, of the variety of new families.

Helen Nestor, 1992

FAMILY PORTRAITS
IN
CHANGING TIMES

Judy Kennedy asked her friend, Paul Quin, to be the father of her child. Paul agreed, with the mutual consent of his partner, Steve Unger, who is now Quin's "Uncle" Steve. Quin Kennedy lives with his mother and visits his father, who lives in another city, on alternate weekends and holidays and half of the summer. Judy is a playwright, Paul is a book designer, and Steve is a software development manager.

Aside from a few friends, my life five years ago was one of a self-absorbed artist. I wanted to open up to a relationship; I wanted to give to someone in an intimate way. This was when I began to think seriously about starting a family. Paul Quin accepted my invitation to co-parent. I have received far more love and support than I could have dreamed. Since the day Quin was born, my life has been filled with love from him, Paul and his family, Steve and his family, several extended families, and a renewed relationship with my own parents. I have, indeed, opened up to the world and have had the world returned to me one hundredfold.

Judy Kennedy

A dozen friends collected over the years are my family. We share ups and downs, help each other out, make life possible and often joyous. Being gay, I didn't take fatherhood fantasies too seriously, but when my friend Judy came to me and my lover Steve about having a child, it took me absolutely no time to say yes.

The totality of parenthood is beyond description. It hit me like a ton of bricks. It is non-negotiable, inconvenient, and forever —at least eighteen years. I hadn't thought about the time that fatherhood would require. Nor that Quin's kindergarten would cost more than my college. I simply didn't think about parenthood changing the friendship Judy and I share.

Especially I wasn't prepared to deal with finding out after Quin was born that I have an AIDS-related condition. Judy and Quin are not infected, but we're all affected. I thought glibly about life lasting forever—until each month became a special dispensation. Judy was freaked out about losing me too soon, and even more that Quin would get infected just being around me. She holds on to Quin tightly; I want lots of time with him.

The anger and fear are hard to deal with—as if Quin's task of growing up weren't difficult enough. But we do okay. Our lives are held together by strong and frequent doses of hope, joy, and family love. Steve and my other friends support us always. Quin is a delight and continually challenges me to be strongly and truly myself—for as many months or years as I can.

Paul Quin

I grew up in a close-knit Jewish family in the suburbs. Every night we discussed our day's activities at the dinner table. My friends were always dazzled by the amount of food my mother stocked in our refrigerator. I grew up expecting that I would become a lawyer, live in the suburbs, have two kids, and join the Temple and a country club.

Funny how life turns out! I went to Yale during the hippie revolution and became a social worker. I'm too near-sighted to drive, so living in the suburbs was out. And I didn't plan on being gay but discovered I was. *Not to worry!* Living in San Francisco has been great, and I *have* joined a synagogue. But I reluctantly gave up on the idea of being a father and raising a family and doubted that Sunday brunch could ever suffice. Then one day Judy called Paul with this wild idea.

Judy had known Paul for some years, but I was a stranger. We became family, but only time and shared experience build friendships. Now, four years later, I am pleased to say that Judy and I are both family *and* friends. Quin visits us every other week. I relish seeing Paul blossom as a father. And I am continually amazed at how Judy manages so much on her own. Most of all, I enjoy being Quin's "Uncle" Steve.

Steve Unger

Judy Kennedy, 39, Paul Quin, 48, Steve Unger, 39, and Judy and Paul's son, Quin Kennedy, four. (1989)

John and Debra Washington work different shifts in order to support their family and care for their children. John works days supervising handicapped workers in a factory, and Debra works nights as a hospital maid.

I first met my husband, John, in October 1976, after I moved to Waukegan, Illinois. My cousin and I were on our way to school and we were late, so she asked John to give us a ride. He did, and that's how we first met. In 1977 John began working as a security guard for a firm across the street from my parents' home. John and my brothers became acquainted, and they became good friends. John was a licensed boxing trainer, and my brothers were interested in it, so he began training them. He would come over every day to pick them up. He and I would speak, and that was it. Later on, one of my brothers began bringing me messages from John telling me that he wanted to know if I would go out with him to dinner, the movies, or concerts. I declined, but John did not stop asking. My brother would try very hard to get me to go out with John. I later found out that he would give Quincy a few dollars to deliver the messages to me. Finally, John gave up and stopped asking. In the meantime, he would visit my parents, brothers, and sisters, and they grew to love John. It was like John was one of the family, so everybody began working on getting me to go to the horse races with him. That was about four years later, and out of the blue I said, "Yes." His dad went also. We had so much fun. From that time on, we began dating and seeing a lot of each other, going places, having a good time. I later met his mom and two sisters, and we all got along fine. His father already knew me because he and my dad were friends. John and I were now the best of friends, and we grew closer. On numerous occasions we would break up, but the breakups never lasted longer than two or three days. He would call, or I would call, and we would be back together. One day, laughing, John said, "We are getting married." So I said, "You didn't ask." He said, "I know; this way you can't say 'no' again." He had asked me twice before.

So we got married, and that's how we came to be. Family is being together no matter what and being there for each other when no one else is. It's taking care of a home, building and growing together. We are teaching our kids and they are teaching us—and we feel silly learning from our kids. It's sacrificing things for each other and getting into arguments on petty things and then being able to still respect each other. It's dreaming of having our own home, not a mansion, just a home in a better neighborhood. We try and save for it and keep hoping, and one day we will be able to get our own home. We have arguments, disagreements, and wonder who's really right and no one giving in till an hour later. I leave the house and say, "I'm not coming back," . . . and about twenty minutes later I'm back. It's discussing the things we want most and planning on how we can try and accomplish them. We want the best for our kids, wondering if we are disciplining them too hard or not

Debra, 26, and John Washington, 34, and their children, Damon, 9, Dakeira, 7, and John III, 5 years old. (1990)

enough—the kids getting angry with us. We know that we will always be there for them. We allow our kids to express themselves to a certain point, whereas when I grew up I would not dare tell my parents what I felt unless I was prepared for a big smack. It was considered then that you were being disrespectful, and if you didn't respect your parents you would practically be disowned.

I would like to see my kids grow up to be very independent, self-supporting, married, very educated, and use what I have taught them over the years. So many parents teach their kids right, yet so many turn around totally different from their upbringing. The most difficult part is trying to keep up with everything that's going on at all times. I think it's important in a family. If I could change anything it would be to further my education before I had kids and have a home of my own to bring them up in a better environment.

Debra Washington

I've been in Waukegan, Illinois, for most of my life. I'm originally from Arkansas. I began in Waukegan boxing programs, and I worked for the city for awhile. After five years of boxing I quit and became a professional boxing trainer. I worked with Mr. Reynaldo Snipes who fought for the world championship against Mr. Larry Holmes. I first met my wife in 1976. Later on, I began training her brothers. I would pick them up and take them to the gym to train. I would see Debra five times a week, but she did not like me then. So I didn't push it. After about seven years of seeing her now and then, we finally got together and we've been together ever since.

I want the best for our kids, but I want them to know you have to work for what you want and earn things, that it does not come by sitting down and doing nothing, and it's not going to be easy. Talking things out makes a good marriage and family, and it also brings each other close. If I could change anything, I would go back to college, take care of my family, and move out of the neighborhood I'm in. This neighborhood is no place to bring up a child. But what keeps me going is the love for my family. It gets hard, but there was also never a promise that it would be easy.

John Washington

Family is Mom and Dad buying me a new bike. I like when we all go to the movies and out to dinner together. My family loves me, but my brother and sister, we still argue a lot. It makes my mom sad, and she spanks us. Sometimes she puts us on punishment, and that's when I wish I was a grownup so no one have to punish me. I like when we play basketball together. I don't know a lot about family, but I know I like mine most of the time.

John Washington III

We do a lot of things together, and Dad plays with us a lot—wrestling, basketball, and boxing. He used to box, and I like this. Him and I talk a lot about drugs. We go to the mall and play arcade games. I don't like it sometimes when I can't go over to my grandma. I don't like doing chores and homework, and Mom says I have to do it, and I get upset and think I don't want a family. I don't like it when I want toys and my mother and dad don't buy them. I am happy when they get home from work. I like my dog, too. And I love to roller-skate. I wish my dad and mom could buy a house some day.

Damon Washington

What I like about my family is they is very, very nice to me, and they treat me right and feed me, too. I have a nice mom and dad, and my brothers and I love my family very much, my Grandma and cousins, especially my baby cousin, Johanna. I don't like whenever my mom don't take me along with her somewhere or she don't let me go outside and she spanks me, it hurts. My mom and dad work and sometimes they come home from work upset, and I don't like it. My family argues, but we never hit one another when arguing. Family should let kids do whatever they want to, but my parents say, "No way."

Dakeira Washington

After living together for two years, Wendy Dutton and Tom Kenny were married in 1987. Their daughter Molly was born in 1990, and their daughter Jesse was born in September 1991. Wendy and Tom call their relationship a "fifty-fifty marriage," sharing parenting, household work, and earning an income. Wendy received an M.F.A. in creative writing in 1990, shortly after the birth of Molly, and teaches critical thinking at a community college. Tom works full time as an editor of a music magazine, and they both share childcare.

Today Molly saw her first butterfly. Last week it was Mozart and macaroni and cheese. I've been a parent eleven months now, and before that I wouldn't even have called us a family. We were more like people on our way to somewhere else.

Tom and I have always had a you-do-your-thing, I'll-do-mine marriage. Pulling together as a family has been comforting and more than a little shocking. The first few months with the baby were so consuming that I felt myself beginning to disappear.

Now Molly has grown more independent, and everything's different. I still don't think of her quite as a human being yet. She's more along the lines of a leprechaun or an Ewok. Being around her has a real feeling of magic.

Even before we were married, Tom and I were committed to the idea of fifty-fifty parenting. That's how crazy idealistic we are. Although Tom does stay with Molly while I teach an early morning English class, I do the bulk of the care during the week while he works full time at a magazine. He does chores and cooks every night. Still, I look forward to some day reversing roles so he can stay home with the kids. Just like I look forward to moving to the country.

So I guess we're still people on our way to somewhere else, but at least we're going there together.

Now I'm pregnant again, and I'm nervous. I don't want Molly's specialness to be diminished. Of course, I'm also concerned about what the hell my day will be like. But then I see other mothers walking by with their kids and I think, "Butterflies, Mozart, macaroni and cheese. I can do this."

Wendy Dutton

Wendy Dutton, 28, and Tom Kenny, 28, and their daughter, Molly Ann Dutton-Kenny, sixteen months old. (1991)

"Even before we were married, Tom and I were committed to the idea of fifty-fifty parenting. That's how crazy idealistic we are."

— *Wendy Dutton*

This Christmas I called back to my parents' house in Indiana. I said to my dad, "I wish I were home for Christmas." He said, "You *are* home." It hadn't hit me until then how far I had come and how rich my life had turned.

I come from a family of twelve children. By the time my mom was my age she had me, her sixth. I can't imagine what that would be like. I remember the house was loud, and sometimes I had two roomates. To me, that was family.

Now we have Molly and another child on the way. Everywhere we go it seems we are the youngest parents. Most of our friends are single. And yet one generation ago we, like our parents, would have been almost done having our family. I feel like we're just getting started.

Welcome to the roller coaster.

Tom Kenny

(Postscript, October 1991)

Sometimes when both girls are sleeping and the house is hushed, it feels like some magic is happening. I find myself just sitting at my desk, listening to their breath. The house is full of them, even in sleep.

Our day goes something like this:

At 6:30, we try to pretend we don't hear Molly awake in her room. Jesse starts crying. While I change and nurse her, my husband works on Molly. We have eggs and oatmeal. Molly throws hers on the floor. I nurse Jesse some more.

After my husband leaves for work at 8:30, there is a great deal of crying and rocking and singing and reading. We go on a walk with the long double stroller and two fat dogs. We are a parade. The neighbors like to see us coming.

After the walk I change each girl. Molly wiggles and kicks and laughs. Jesse screams. She wets her outfit and has to be re-dressed. I nurse her again while Molly plays. I eat a sandwich. I do everything one-handed.

Now it's Molly's turn, but she refuses to sit in her high chair. I chase her around the house with spoonfuls of refried beans. I give up and do the dishes, make the bed. In the background I listen to a soap opera as if it were radio.

After lunch the three of us lie on the bed, watching the spiders on the ceiling. Molly chugs a bottle and insists we read *Go, Dog. Go!* three times. After I carry Molly to her crib, I pick up all the toys and books. I take a shower. I change and nurse Jesse again.

My husband calls for the third time. He asks me to defrost the chicken. He tells me there is a rumor going around work that Jesse looks like a hedgehog. I assure him she is more along the lines of Jackie Gleason.

By 2:00, Molly is awake and we hit the deck in the backyard. I fill up the children's pool for Molly and nurse in the shade. Molly comes over with a bucket of water and dumps it in my lap on Jesse. Later she attacks my ponytail through the slats of the chair.

I lie to my friends. "No, Molly's not jealous," I say over the phone. "She just loves Jesse." And it is true she says her name and kisses her and pets her and only smacks occasionally.

One of my friends calls dinnertime "the witching hour." Molly whines for her dad's attention. He is making dinner, I am nursing. While our hands are full, Molly comes around and bites our legs. "It's a bad time for grown-ups, too," my mother-in-law informs me. "Why do you think they have happy hours?"

When we sit down, there is more food throwing. I start Molly's bathwater and let her run around naked while we finish eating. Molly scampers past, looking sheepish. I tell my husband I think she has pooped somewhere, but where?

Then suddenly everything is different. Molly is in the bathtub. Jesse is back asleep. I listen to Molly splashing her dad while I do the dishes. Then I pick up the toys and books and pots and pans and empty bottles for the last time. The dogs are quiet.

I collapse on the couch and take the tally of the day: I yelled twice. I ignored Jesse's crying once. I didn't know the endings to any of the songs I sang. I forgot to pet the cat.

And then there are the good things: Molly crawled on her hands and knees and barked like a dog. Jesse seemed to smile. I remembered to water the houseplants.

Wendy Dutton

Marcia and Ricardo Hofer and their daughter Jennifer, were first photographed shortly before the birth of their second daughter, Amy. At that time, Ricardo was working as a psychologist and Marcia was a homemaker and university student. Now both Marcia and Ricardo work as psychologists, sharing an office as well as the care of their home and the care and rearing of Jennifer and Amy. When the family was photographed again in 1989, Jennifer was home from college for the holidays.

In some ways, the family I came from was quite different from the one I've created. What comes to mind first is the number of us: I have three younger brothers, so the potential for chaos, noise, and commotion was multiplied tremendously. And there was quite a lot of fighting among us—some of it physical, some of it battles of nerves, so it was a relief to me that my kids have gotten along so well. Having just two children, and having them so far apart in age, certainly has made for a calmer life than my parents had, I think, and enabled us to spend more time with the kids. Of course, there's always a trade-off: while I would've happily done without some of the pandemonium that characterized my first family, I'm absolutely crazy about my brothers now and love having a large family. In fact, family gatherings have been some of our happiest times.

Another difference, which has to do with the times, is that my dad was the professional and chief breadwinner, and although my mom was extremely bright, she'd had less education, having grown up in an immigrant family where the resources went to educate her brother. She did have some part-time jobs, but not what we'd call a career today. Interestingly enough, I don't have the feeling that she thought any less of herself because of this. Of course, most women of that generation didn't expect to have careers beyond raising their families, but I suspect that many of them were frustrated, and I never had that sense about my mom.

Then there were some differences that had to do with hard times. My folks had a rough time making ends meet during much of my childhood, and I think that was very stressful for them—I certainly remember it. Having gone through a similar period in the early years of our marriage, I can understand now how hard it must have been for my parents. Also, my mom developed cancer in her late 30s, and died of it ten years later. She had a long period of remission, and my parents tried to shield us as much as they could from the impact, but of course it affected all of us.

There are some similarities, too. Although Ricardo and my dad are very different in temperament, my stepmother and I often joke about how alike they are. Ricardo has always been actively involved in the day-to-day activities of the family; that's not so unusual in our generation, but I think he's involved to an unusual degree. He sews and I don't, so he's the one that made curtains and figured out how to make a dog costume for Halloween. And my dad was quite atypical for his generation in that respect. I remember him washing dishes, cooking Sunday breakfasts, and bathing us when we were little. (Actually, we used to dread his energy and thoroughness, especially as a hair-washer!)

Humor is really dominant in both families—a lot of good-natured teasing is part of it, and I'm often teased by my kids in a way that's reminiscent of the way we used to tease my mom, and about the same kinds of things. And then there are the hilarious things that happen and become part of family lore, which in both families get pulled out and enjoyed over and over again..

Most of all, I think that the basic values are quite similar. People often ask Ricardo and me about the cross-cultural aspect of our marriage, since I was born in the U.S. and Ricardo is from Argentina. Of course it's a factor, but since we're both from an Eastern European Jewish background, in many ways our families were more similar than different. So our way of thinking about the world and people has always had a lot in common, and of course that's influenced the family we've created together.

I've had the luxury of being able to structure my career, whether it was school or work, around the children as much as I felt I needed to. So I never felt I had much of a problem balancing career and family, because my basic decision was that I wasn't going to have my kids pay a price for my desire for a career. (That was my goal; the kids may or may not feel that I achieved it.) Psychology is a second career for me, and since Ricardo was already established in the field when I decided to enter it, he took on the responsibility of providing financial stability, and I spent more time with the kids and organizing the household. But we've always shared parenting completely in terms of decision-making and emotional involvement.

When I think of my fondest memories of the family, many of them are from the time when the children were little. Maybe there's a natural tendency to remember the good times in the past more clearly than the difficult ones, but I enjoyed them tremendously as babies, and they were both, in very different ways, adorable little kids. I also think of how exciting it was to see them develop and become independent people, which of course they're still in the process of doing. Some of our best times as a family have been the times when we're relaxed together, when our particular brand of humor, which is very funny but also expresses a great deal of affection, comes into play. I don't think it's accidental that the two portraits catch us in moments of humor. In the first, Jennifer had been clowning around, and Ricardo had said jokingly, "Can't you be serious for just one minute?" So what was caught in the photograph was her mock-serious expression. And in the second photo it's the two kids who are clowning together.

The most important change in our family in the time between the first and second photos, of course, is that in the second one Amy is very much a presence. I'm sure that for any family the arrival of a second child causes all kinds of changes. But when I think about Amy, what comes to mind is how much we've enjoyed her, with her quirky sense of humor (even as a baby), her inquisitive mind, and her quiet but solid sense of who she is. And of course Jennifer is bound up in this, too, because part of what feels so satisfying to me about having two kids is the relationship they have with each other and how much they love each other. Ricardo and I have always felt that the six years between the girls had a lot to do with this—Jennifer had already had a big dose of our love and attention by the time Amy was born and had school and friends in her life. So she didn't seem to feel threatened by having a baby sister, and the two of them developed a very affectionate relationship right from the start. I guess what I'm saying is that it isn't just the parents that do the parenting when it comes to the younger child, and I think that some of Amy's good feeling about herself must have come from Jennifer's capacity to accept her into the family.

The two photos capture us before and after important family milestones: at the time of the first, Amy was about to arrive on the scene, and at the time of the second, Jennifer had just spent her first semester away at college. So at the earlier time we were dealing with all the feelings that adding a child to the family brings up, and at the later time it was somewhat the reverse, as we had to get used to not having Jennifer at home. For me it was a mix of feelings: at

first, a house that seemed unnaturally quiet and neat, worrying about whether she was eating and sleeping enough, missing her, but at the same time feeling excited for her and tremendously proud. Of course, she's still very much a part of the family, but it feels to me that having a child leave home is a new developmental phase, for the family as a unit and for me individually. It's not just that it feels different, and sometimes easier, to have one child in the house; without Jennifer here, Amy suddenly seemed older and bigger—less our adorable mascot and more a kid on the verge of adolescence. And I find myself thinking ahead to the time that Amy will leave, too, and that then the hands-on part of being parents, which is something that Ricardo and I have done very much together, will be over for us. And that makes me feel both sad and excited, because it will involve a loss, but also a great deal of freedom for us.

When I was pregnant with Jennifer, I found it hard to imagine having a girl, since the babies in my family were all boys. But I've loved having daughters; it's nice to see them growing up feeling good about their intelligence and feeling that they don't have to limit their choices or interests because they're female— that wasn't the case as much for my generation. I do think this is a difficult time for young women. So much is open to them, and that's exciting, yet as a society we haven't solved the problems parents face in having careers and children. Of course, this is only one of the problems we haven't solved, but it's one that I worry about for my own children. Will they have the choices I had about spending time with their families? My hopes for them are that they find something to do with their lives that they enjoy and that's meaningful for them and that they have loving relationships.

Marcia Hofer

I like this opportunity to show the side of our family that can keep a sense of humor even in the face of a task that is not necessarily pleasant (some of us are realistic about our looks; some of us better be.) I consider this a strength in our family, and something that did not change from the first sitting, since the photograph that was chosen then also captured a moment of having fun, of hilarity. The most obvious change is that the child that was then inside of Marcia is now very much outside and just as much her own person, but again the continuity: she is perhaps the greatest source of humor in our family.

I came from an intact nuclear family, as did Marcia. Thus, I suppose that it was inevitable that the family we created together would encompass all the tensions inherent in this particular form of family living,

Marcia, 35, and Ricardo Hofer, 37, and their daughter, Jennifer, 6 years old. (1977)

*Marcia and Ricardo Hofer
and their daughters Jennifer,
17, and Amy, 11 years old.
(1989)*

"On the dark side, I feel that the world is not very hospitable to the raising of children....I had to teach them about the Holocaust, and then they could not be spared the learning of history, nor their seeing how shabbily we treat the poor, the weak, and the ill."

— Ricardo Hofer

and in that the two families, the one of origin and my current one, have much of a common ground. In addition, some of the important personal issues and themes are common in both: my parents were immigrants, as I am (although I had it considerably easier than my parents did, and I tried as hard as I could to make it even easier on my children); both families have tremendous respect for and liking of learning; work and responsibility are much valued; we have a great interest and concern for social issues and causes; both families share a rather jaundiced and skeptical outlook on the world and its people.

There are also differences between the two families. I believe that our current family has a much brighter and lighter feel to it. We are much freer in our thinking and feeling and, particularly, in their expression among ourselves than was true in my family of origin. The kind of teasing that my children engage in with both Marcia and me would have been inconceivable with my parents. We are also much more expressive emotionally than my parents were. I have been much more involved in the day-to-day dealings with my children than my father was with his. Another important difference is that there has been an almost complete absence of sibling rivalry between my children, in sharp contrast to the situation with my sisters when we were young. Finally, I think that we treated our children as full-fledged persons at a much earlier age than my parents did.

I often felt that I did not have enough time with my family, even though I know that statistically I spent much more time with them than the average professional male does. In terms of my particular profession (psychotherapist), there have been some specific and peculiar problems: confidentiality forced me to be cautious in talking to my children about my work, particularly since living in a small community, they might have known some of the people I was working with. Another fallout of being a psychotherapist is that as soon as my children figured out what work I did, they became highly suspicious that I was "analyzing" them and reacted to that quite negatively (they also used it at times as a rationalization to get away with murder, of course). On the positive side, they could see me engaged in productive work, with a social value, interesting to me and challenging.

There are too many fond memories of raising our family to even attempt to list them. I enjoyed my children's babyhoods tremendously and the bonding that occurred at this time. Then I loved the explosion of interest, curiosity and mastery of their first years of life. Then their slow, but definite coming into their own personhood.

On the dark side, I feel that the world is not very hospitable to the raising of children. At the societal level, I had to teach them about the Holocaust, and then they could not be spared the learning of history (carnage upon carnage), nor their seeing how shabbily we treat the poor, the weak, and the ill. At a more personal level, it has pained me no end at what young age they had to learn to protect themselves from the aggression and haywire sexuality that surround us. Now that they are older, it saddens me that they have to be ever so much more cautious about experimenting, with the prevalence of sexually transmitted diseases, drugs, and kookiness. I just hope they come out whole.

As I look at these photographs of our family, I relish the idea that they enlarge the limited and precarious extent of our memories. I am moved by the probability that these photographs will evoke thoughts and feelings in my great-grandchildren, whatever they may be, much as the single extant photograph of my paternal grandfather, whom I never knew, evokes in me.

Having written the above, I realize it embodies some of those things that I wish to impart to my children: the cherishing of the strong and complex bonds made and forged in the context of family relations; a great regard for memory, both personal and social; a sense of humor no matter what.

Ricardo Hofer

In some ways, my family is a paradox. By societal standards, my family is "normal:" my parents are together, they have two kids, they both have jobs, etcetera. Yet when we attempt to attach the word "normal" to the words "Hofer family" we cannot keep a straight face. And that's one of my favorite things about my family. When we are together we bring out the silliness in each other and hilarity abounds.

When I was younger and not getting along with my parents too well, I worried that if I were not their daughter and I met them somehow, I would not like them as people. Luckily, my angry feelings did not reflect reality. One of the most pleasant things about my family is that each person in it is an individual (most often a rather strange and most definitely stubborn individual), and I love the other three individuals to pieces. Especially after I moved out of the house and got a bit more perspective on the family

scene, I began to appreciate what fantastic people my parents and my sister are. You see, you caught me at a good moment: I'm home from college on winter break, and I'm getting along great with my family. I can't think of anything I'd change about it. However, had I been asked to write this a mere year or two ago, perhaps I would have raved a bit less. But now I find my mother's nagging funny and my father's (sometimes) bullheadedness admirable and that my sister is growing up to be one incredible (if mildly bizarre) woman..

Jennifer Hofer

My family may be annoying, cheerful, quiet, and telephone-dominating at times, but it is, above all, unique. One of the best aspects of my family is our sense of humor. There is always teasing and joking going on, lightening the atmosphere, and not only is it managed to be incorporated into nearly every discussion, but normal jokes are always vetoed on the spot and immediately crammed down the teller's throat.

Both of my parents work, yet I don't feel deprived of time spent with them. When I was about 5 I remember my mom writing her dissertation, and that took up some time, but because she has not been working full time, she has been home a lot. I did see less of my dad, however, because of the demands of his work. I think that they have balanced their time very well—I certainly wouldn't want to be around them all the time! Problems with them have arisen because we live with each other, and because they have the authority over my life. However, I feel that none of these problems are unsolvable, and I see my family in a positive light. Overall, I would not trade my family. And if I was stupid enough to, I would be missing out on a lot.

Amy Hofer

In 1965, Rose Linsky chose to become a mother and gave birth to her daughter, Jessica. As a single parent, Rose worked full time as a teacher to support herself and Jessica. Rose is now a retired high-school teacher, and Jessica recently graduated from college and works in a retail store.

In 1965 I was a 33-year-old, unmarried schoolteacher suffering from what are now called the imperatives of the biological clock. For some years I had wanted to marry. I was suffering too from the malaise that probably comes to everyone in what Dante described as "the middle of the journey." I longed to be fruitful and multiply, to participate in the joys and griefs of family, to have someone to love. I decided, married or not, to have a baby. I had a tenured position, so I could support both of us, if I managed not to offend the sensibilities of the school district. I hoped, rather unrealistically, that the father would gallantly insist on marriage. Instead, he wanted nothing to do with me or my child. To him I must have been a "loose woman.". We did not know each other well or long, and today only my daughter knows the name of her biological father.. She has always known how we came to be a family, but at my school a more socially acceptable account had to be presented. So I announced that I was to be married and applied for a year's leave of absence.

From the beginning I had the approval and the blessing of my closest friends, one a colleague at school and the other a lawyer whom I had known since we were sophomores. They were both married mothers, and they included me in family get-togethers and in holiday celebrations. Because of them I felt protected and cherished, very much a part of the community. When I went to see my father and to tell him I was pregnant, I had no idea of how he would take the news. To my great astonishment and relief, he was overjoyed. He told me that he was delighted and thoroughly approved. His response was the greatest gift I have ever received.

I loved being pregnant, preparing for what was then called "natural childbirth" and meditating on possible names. I asked myself what woman, living or dead, fictional or mythical, I would choose to be a model of female virtue. I chose Portia in Merchant of Venice. She was wise and beautiful, pure and dutiful. She was supremely capable, and she was obedient to the wishes of her dead father. Best of all, her father had provided her with a superb way to choose a mate.

(Remember the riddle of the three caskets.) I began to reread the play. Other children, I feared, would confuse Portia with Porche. So I chose, instead, the name Jessica—after Shylock's daughter, a woman of ambiguous character, a rebel with a Colonial American sounding name meaning "beloved of God."

Now, at 22 years of age, Jessica embodies Portia's wisdom, beauty, and courage, as well as her namesake's rebellion. I had a hard time forgiving her for growing up. Perhaps because there were only two of us, the separation necessary for adolescents was particularly painful, like birth itself. I look back at those troubles now with serenity, but I sometimes think they might never have been, had I been true to myself and called her Portia. I hope that eventually my daughter will have children and that she will marry before she has them. Whatever happens, I hope to give her the encouragement and the approval my father gave to me.

Rose Linsky

Dear Mom,

Growing up with you was hard. Our relationship was difficult and often filled with anger. But I do not regret our past because it helped form me. Today I love myself just as I love you.

We lived in such close and constant contact that our expectations of each other became unrealistically high. I resented you for wanting a perfect daughter, while refusing to forgive you for not being a perfect parent.

I think that time apart has allowed us to develop ourselves independently of one another, and also allowed us to see each other's beauty and strength. I hope you will forgive me for the difficulties I have caused you, just as I have forgiven you.

Love always,
Jessica

Rose Linsky, 57, and her daughter, Jessica Linsky, 22. (1989)

Juan and Maria Gonzalez emigrated to the United States from Jalisco, Mexico, when they married in 1982. They had planned to work for a year, save money to buy a house, and then return to Mexico. Instead, they have remained in the U.S., living and working on a horse ranch in Northern California. Their three children were born in the U.S. Their statements were compiled from a recorded interview in Spanish.

I grew up on a ranch near Jalos, Mexico, taking care of cows. I liked my work and I had the opportunity to spend all that time milking cows. We were five brothers and six sisters. We all worked there, but I ended up alone because, as they got older, they got married and went on to other things. I'm the middle child, but I was the last to marry. They all married before me because my wife, Maria, was waiting for me. *(Maria responds, "No, it was the other way around; he was waiting for me because I was still a little girl.")*

I remember myself as a child playing marbles. I always had something to do. We didn't have any real problems. My parents used to work the land and harvest corn and beans and get all together to provide for the house. It was the same, year after year. After awhile, my dad dug a well, and that changed his life. The land was transformed through irrigation. Everything was very different because we had a lot of water. Before that I used to bring the water in a truck from wherever I could find it. I don't live there anymore, but now the harvest is bigger and they have diversified what they plant. It's not the same as before when they used oxen to plow the field. Now they have a tractor.

The first job I had wasn't that difficult. I worked with the horses for six months, and then I moved to work at a ranch with the cows. So I had to get up earlier. Maria had to be alone because I was busy. She said she was unhappy, but I was very busy, and that's how we had to be. I have had work the whole time. I never spent a month unemployed. I never had problems because I couldn't understand. I was here, no problem; I went to Arizona, no problem; I came back here, no problem. So really, I don't know. Here people are envious of me because I just always had work.

My wife and I agree on everything. We like the same things and we cooperate to keep things together so we don't have differences. She cooks the way they cook in Mexico, so there isn't any difference in what we eat. We live as a family as if we were living in Mexico. Outside it's different, but we always go out together, so I don't notice any real difference.

I have a wonderful relationship with my kids. I spend a lot of time just playing with them. When I am here they are around me most of the time. When I have to work, sometimes they come with me for a while and

Juan, 49, and Maria Guadalupe Gonzalez, 37, and their children, Marta, 7, Hugo, 3, and Liliana, 2. (1990)

"What do we hope for our children? We have a lot of hopes. We really want to give them the best."

— *Juan Gonzalez*

then go back home. I get along very well in my work; I can do my work and then come home. I like my work because there isn't anything else. If there were something better, maybe it would be better, but that's not the case, so I have to deal with this.

When I was working on this ranch part time before, there used to be some problems with the workers. When I came here, yes, there were also some problems, but now everything is okay. I have been here for almost three years now. What do I hope for our children? We have a lot of hopes. We really want to give them the best.

Juan Gonzalez

In Mexico we grew up happy, content, with no needs, but yes with many desires for things that we couldn't have. I'm from Jalisco, from "Jalos." There wasn't much money then and our family was large. There were fifteen of us, but we ended up with nine...the others died.

My father got sick when I was 6 years old. Something was wrong with his lungs, and he spent six years in a chair without being able to move for anything. I don't remember it well, but my mother said he gave us his blessing, said goodbye to us, and left us because no doctor could figure out what was wrong with him because it was an infection of the lungs, tuberculosis. It's a disease that was contagious for the family. He went to Jalos and we stayed on the ranch so that he could live away from us.

My father got the address of this doctor in Guadalajara, but he didn't have much hope anymore because all the doctors said there was no cure. But he went to Guadalajara and the doctor said, "I'm going to lay hands on you (cure you), but you are going to do what I say, otherwise I won't even try to lay hands on you." My father said, "I will do whatever you say, but tell me that I can still live with my family." The doctor said, "You can stay with your family, but you are going to do what I say. The very first thing, you have to quit cigarettes and alcohol, (my father didn't drink, but he told him anyway) and soda and you cannot work." My father said, "I have my young children," but the doctor said, "You can't work."

So my father could come back home. I was 6 then, and my father was only about 50, still young. He spent six years in treatment, sitting in his chair without moving anywhere for anything. After six years, he was better. They told him he could work again, but he still couldn't work because he was so fat and he had bronchitis, too. He did work some, but very little. Even then, while I was still a child I had to start sewing. I don't know if you've seen women in Mexico making blouses. Instead of playing, I was sewing to make money for his medicine and to eat. All of us sewed, except the two boys; they farmed.

Our childhood in Mexico had its difficulties, but we were happy, even though we were poor. My father was the owner of the ranch, so we lived and worked on our ranch. I was in charge of the stable, and we milked about ten cows. I went to school for only about two years at the ranch, my brothers and sisters too. Two or three years was the most any of us studied. We couldn't go to town because there wasn't any transportation and we had to work. When I was a child, I really wanted to go to school. When my father was better, I told him I wanted to go to school with my sister. I was about 12, and my father said, "No, you're not going to go because you fight a lot with Lupe" (my niece). "You're not going to go. Dumb little donkeys in heaven are worth more than lawyers in hell." My father always had that in his mind, so there were two strong reasons why he didn't let me study. I was the youngest in the house so I had to help everyone. I'm the baby. I have sisters who are in their 50s; Juanita is already 60. I'm the little one, but now I'm old too.

My mother's family is very big. She has fifty-eight grandchildren and sixty great-grandchildren from her nine children. Seven are married, and two are nuns. Of the oldest, one has fourteen children, one has twelve and another eleven. There are four of us here [in the U.S.]. The others have only come for visits. In 1979, I came to the U.S. for the first time for a visit. I was still single, and I stayed with my sister and worked in Santa Ana, California. I came because I wanted to earn my own money. I came for the season and worked and made money, and then I went back with my parents. My parents came back sometimes with me later, and then they went back, or we all went back to Mexico together. I met my husband because we are from the same town. My husband is older, and he met me when I was still a little girl. We knew of each other because our families were very

connected. Two of my sisters are married with two brothers and one of their sisters is my husband's sister-in-law. So we were acquaintances, we knew each other, but we weren't really friends.

I don't know how, but Juan tricked me and he brought me to the U.S. Well, I don't know who tricked who. Maybe it's better to say I tricked him. It's a mystery. We were married in 1982, and we thought we would come to the U.S. for one year to work and save money to buy a house. We thought one year was enough to buy a house. But ten years later, we're still here. We did buy a house in Jalos, but we stayed here. Juan's parents lived in the house. Now it is just his mother in the house because his father died. We don't know when that year will be over. It's been a very long year, because we now have three children and another one on the way and who knows when. Our oldest daughter is already in school, and our son starts next month, one day a week, because he is already 5. Then next year, he'll go every day. We like it here. We live comfortably on the ranch.

Raising a family in the U.S. is different from Mexico in every way. In Jalos, we grew up very connected to the church. Here, that's not possible because of Juan's work and the lack of transportation. So in that way it's very different. Economically, my children have it very different than we did growing up in Mexico. It's much easier to stay in school in the U.S. than it is in Mexico. For me, in every sense it is very different. In Mexico you have to buy everything for school, from pencils to books. Here, you don't. Here everything is easier—transportation and lunches. In Mexico, everything comes out of your pocket. So, for a parent, it's more difficult in Mexico than here for school.

As far as the church, I liked it better the way I was raised in Mexico. Here it's not as easy because you

> *"Raising a family in the U.S. is different from Mexico in every way....I think everything is easier in the U.S. for a family and for the parents."*
>
> — *Maria Guadalupe Gonzalez*

need a car for everything and there are not as many churches or a cathedral or as many services. Jalos is a small town, and the church is close, so everyone can walk, and there are many services.

I think everything is easier in the U.S. for a family and for the parents. Our home life today in the U.S. is about the same as when Juan and I were growing up in Mexico. We have the same customs and the same rules. The only thing that's different is that when we grew up in Mexico we used a lot of very simple tools to work around the house, to make tortillas, or to iron clothes. In the U.S. that's not necessary, everything is easier. Here you have a stove, electricity—you don't have to be on your knees washing your clothes in the river. In Mexico, we had to wash our clothes in the river and then iron them with little charcoal-heated irons. So in that sense, it is more comfortable in the U.S. But our way of living, our customs, are about the same.

When we first came here we had a very hard time. Everything was so hard because at first they said the work was ready. That was a lie. At the house, when we arrived, the first few weeks everything was okay, very nice. In later weeks, things were not okay when Juan went to work. I spent three days almost without food. A neighbor gave me food, she gave me one taco a day. We had all kinds of problems, people looking down on us. We didn't know anything. We didn't know where to go to look for a job because we didn't have a car. We didn't know that there were Mexican workers on all of the ranches. We didn't speak the language. So we suffered a lot. That's why we want our children to learn about Mexico, too. Maybe one day they will have to leave and we won't be here to help them. We don't want them to have to suffer through what we have already done. Our children have to be ready to face life here *and* there.

We also want them to get to know our family. Here they know just a few of them because most of our relatives are in Mexico. We don't miss them so much anymore. We're more accustomed to the isolation here. When I arrived in the U.S. I cried a lot. I was very sad. I felt very lonely when Juan got his first job. I didn't have a radio or television. I didn't know any of the other wives or any of the other workers. I didn't know anything. Juan left for work at three in the morning and then came back for lunch, and then he had to work here on the horse ranch. So I spent the whole day alone because my first girl was just a baby. It was very sad. I cried a lot. But now it's fine. I've gotten used to it. I was accustomed to working in factories with lots of people when I came to this country. When I was in Mexico, I worked in stores. Being alone so much here I thought that I was going to swallow my tongue and just not be able to talk anymore.

Juan's English is not very good, and without English, you don't work. But so far nothing has happened. People say that Juan always has a smile on his face, so the employers are very happy with him because they say that he respects them and does the work very well. We don't have a great car; we don't have money; the employers don't give us a great house; but we are happy because they always support us. Before us, they used to change workers very often. In our case, the employers asked us to come back from Arizona, and we haven't had any problems since. Now I understand a little English. So in case they have a misunderstanding or they want to talk to Juan they come over here, and we work it out with hand signals or with the English that they think I speak. We understand each other. Now they are taking Spanish lessons because they want to talk and understand Juan. All of the horses here have different owners who rent space for them. Before it was a problem because everyone who came to work here thought that the owner was the only one who would give them orders. It's not that way. All the owners of the horses are bosses and give orders. So one says one thing, another says another thing.

On a normal day, I get up to make breakfast and Juan gets up to go to work. Then he comes back, and we have breakfast together and talk, and he plays with the kids. I clean the house. It's a routine we have all of the time. We always go everywhere together. If I go to the doctor, we go together. We also shop together. I am now taking Marta to catechism, and we go together. We never go out alone, neither of us. So I think that we are very united in the family. If there are any problems, economically or anything, we never keep secrets from each other, we always come to an agreement.

As a married woman I have never worked outside of the house, although some people have offered me jobs as a dishwasher three days a week, but Juan didn't let me. He asked who would have taken care of the kids? We would have had to pay somebody to take care of them. So at the end it would have been the same, and they wouldn't have been with their mother.

We support each other in everything. Juan helps me the way one helps another. We are always happy, content, we are the way we are, and we are happy. The worst times have been when we've had to separate, when my father died and when his father died. Those were the only times we were apart. Other than that, we've been very happy. Those times were very difficult and very sad, but it was God's will, and you have to accept it. We have many hopes for our children, but who knows if they will do it. We try to make sure they study and learn so they can do better for their good, and for our good, too. But who knows. I hope they do well as they grow up, that they respond the way we expect. Life is hard no matter what.

We want to take our children to Mexico for awhile so that they can learn our language well and Mexican culture. So they can learn a little bit of everything there. The problem is that we don't know when. I have had some problems with immigration with my papers. But yes, we would like to take them for six months or a year or two. It's hard to say for how long. We want to take them for awhile so that they understand about both cultures. Because if one day, for some reason, they have to leave here, we don't want them to suffer, to struggle in the way we have. Now we are established and comfortable. We know how to live here.

Maria Guadalupe Gonzalez

Daniel W. and Pastora Gandor, their son, Daniel J., and Daniel W.'s mother, Josephine Gandor, live together. When the Gandors first married in 1979, they chose to live with Daniel W.'s mother in her home, the house where Daniel W. grew up. Pastora emigrated from Cuba to the United States in 1969. Josephine was born in the United States to parents who were Polish immigrants. Her husband, who is deceased, was also born in Poland. Daniel W. has recently received his Ph.D. in biology and is in a two-year forensic science training program in serology with the state police. Pastora works in a bakery. Josephine is a retired bookkeeper.

A family, like any social structure, is always difficult to characterize because it represents a very dynamic interrelationship between the individuals who comprise it. Accordingly, defining one's role within the family is equally difficult because it also is dynamic in that it constantly changes as situations warrant. This is particularly true of families such as mine, which are inclusive of more than just the nuclear unit of father, mother, and children.

My wife, Pastora, my 11-year-old son, Daniel J., and I live with my mother in the same one-family house in which I grew up on the northwest side of Chicago. Even before Pastora and I were married in 1979, we made the decision to live with my mom for a number of reasons, none of which was financial. I lived with my mom before I was married and continued living with her after I was married because I felt it was wrong to leave her alone at this time in her life. Within a period of just five years (1968-1973), she had lost her sister, her only brother, and her husband (my father). My mother has always been a family person, never really too independent or a loner. I remember what a devastating effect those losses had on her and still have on her, and I felt I could make these latter years of her life happier by staying here. Even though both my brother and my sister (along with their families) live in the Chicago area and keep in close contact with Mom, I believe that my remaining here with my family, especially a growing son, has done a lot to keep her spirits high and keep her active in family affairs on a day-to-day basis.

At first, one may cringe at the thought of having a mother and daughter-in-law living under the same roof—much less a son and grandson. And understandably, there do arise very definite conflicts of interest when living under such an arrangement, as you may well imagine. But it is surprising how much one can learn about others and about oneself if one is willing to exercise the care and concern necessary to make such complicated relationships work. The key word here is "willing," and fortunately I have been blessed with a wife and mother who are just that.

The greatest conflicts in living with my mother arise almost exclusively when what she sees as her responsibility to her son overlaps with what my wife sees as her responsibility to her husband. This can range from cooking meals and cleaning clothes to giving advice (requested or not) and directing attention. Over the years, each has learned to recognize each other's limits and together they have really achieved a nice working mutual respect for each other.

Another conflict arises, not surprisingly, from the age difference. As young parents raising a very active child, we do things quickly, whether it be shopping or

Pastora, 34, and Daniel W. Gandor, 37, their son, Daniel J., 11, and Josephine Gandor, 77, Daniel W.'s grandmother. (1990)

> *"If the primary purpose of a family is to provide a warm and loving environment in which the young can grow, the old can relax, and everyone can enjoy, then I truly believe we are doing fairly well."*
>
> — *Josephine Gandor*

eating meals or getting ready for work in the mornings. Naturally, my mom, who is approaching 80 years of age and is suffering quite badly from arthritis in the knees, moves much more slowly. In and of itself this is not a problem, but occasionally impatience can arise on either our part or hers and it can lead to misunderstandings. Finally, it is well known that grandparents spoil children and parents discipline them. Frequently these two principles are diametrically opposed to one another. But again, over the years things have worked out.

Throughout these past eleven years, I believe each of us had learned to be more patient and tolerant with one another, more understanding of each other, and above all, more genuinely concerned about the needs of the other. Whether love enables one to work towards such an understanding and concern, or whether love is born as a result of it, I'm not certain. I am certain, however, that love grows and deepens because of it. Our years of living together as a family have given me a new dimension of respect for my mother, a deeper appreciation and admiration for my wife, and an indescribable feeling of closeness and happiness with my son.

I feel my home has always been, and will always be, an environment that nurtures the growth and development of each individual member through the support and encouragement of others. And I believe a large part of this individual growth comes from the realization and appreciation of how important each of the others was in this growth process. It is the basis upon which all solid families are built—and it is just such a family that I am proud and thankful to be involved with..

Daniel W. Gandor

When I think of the Gandor family, many wonderful thoughts run through my mind. Through all the years I dated Daniel, I was moved by how much love and warmth was generated within that household.

When I moved in after we were married, I hoped that love would grow deeper, and it did. Not only did I learn to love my mother-in-law, but I also learned to respect her for her wisdom, through which I have learned to be a better wife and mother when our son was born. She has always been there for us when we needed her, giving us moral support, encouragement or just a simple helping hand throughout our married life. Needless to say, I have also learned a lot about how to cook from her. She has even attempted to teach me the art of crocheting, but I am absolutely no good at it.

We really do not have too many conflicts in living together because my mother-in-law is a very easy-going person and is not difficult to get along with. If anything, it is my own little quirks that emerge, but she is very smart and very wise and knows when to let matters be.

As far as conflicts over raising Daniel Joseph, I would say there aren't any really, because she always asks before doing something concerning him. She does not take the middle ground between my husband and me and Daniel Joseph. She has given him much love, affection, and wisdom throughout his 11 years.

I feel great pride in seeing our son grow day by day into a warm, intelligent, and caring young man. I pray that he continues to grow this way forever. With my husband I have learned the beauty of love and understanding, for he is a very good-natured man. Every morning I wake up next to him and thank God for sending me an angel from heaven and for making me a part of this family of which I am so very proud. We have a strong bond that unites all of us, and I would never consider changing a thing in my life, for I am happier than I ever imagined I could be.

Pastora Gandor

Having an extended family living under one roof is something I have been used to all my life. When I was a child growing up, my maternal grandfather lived with us (my mother, father, three sisters, one brother, and myself) until I was about 10 years of age, whereupon he returned to Poland to be with his family. Soon afterwards came the Depression, and while we continued to grow up with only the bare necessities, we all had plenty of love to share with one another. Eventually my brother, sisters, and I got married and had our own families, but we continued to stay in close contact with one another.

After the death of my mother, my father came to live with my husband and me and our two children at the time for several years, until he died. He was loved and missed by us all. So as you can see, living together with my son, daughter-in-law, and grandson does not at all seem an unusual living arrangement to me. Quite the contrary, I feel I have been blessed in having all of us living together as a family. It has been wonderful to watch and enjoy my grandson grow from a baby into a handsome and brilliant young lad of 11 years. I cherish these memories that are so precious to me.

Perhaps the most difficult part of my situation is the use of good judgment and discretion in dealing with differences of opinion concerning family matters. I try to avoid taking sides or interfering in those issues best left decided between my son and his wife. I believe the motto "Live and let live" is good to live by because everyone has their own hopes and aspirations in life. My hopes for all my children are for them to lead happy, successful, and most of all, self-fulfilling lives.

If the primary purpose of a family is to provide a warm and loving environment in which the young can grow, the old can relax, and everyone can enjoy, then I truly believe we are doing fairly well.

Josephine Gandor

When any person would ask me what one thing is unique about my family, I would always answer the same. The family itself is unique. First of all, it's nice having two grandmothers from different backgrounds that influence me in different but good ways. I get to try a lot of special foods, too.

Growing up with different cultural backgrounds has broadened my view of the world. They have influenced me by showing some of the different customs of some countries. Because of this, I appreciate the nationalities of my fellow classmates. Also, I love having two wonderful parents like mine. They are so kind and lovable towards me. They help me do homework, answer my questions, and teach me many things. In addition to that, both my parents and grandparents together teach me the greatest knowledge—the knowledge of love and respect.

Having an extra parent has been sometimes complicated because one person will say, "Do this," while the other one says, "Do that." I sometimes don't know what to do. Usually, though, I follow what my parents say because they know me the best.

If I could change anything or anybody in this family, it would be myself. I think I would change because sometimes I forget to show my love and respect for them. I wouldn't want to change the other members of my family because I think they're perfect the way they are.

The one word that I think could describe my family would be, troop. Troop is the perfect word because I think of my family as one loving and respectable unit. Also, there is one word I always remember when I look at my family, "wysiwyg" (what you see is what you get), so I always see the best, and that must mean I have the best.

Daniel Joseph Gandor

Michele and Alfred Williams met in high school and married about seven years later. After graduation, Michele became a full-time mother and homemaker. She plans to continue her education and work outside the home when her children are older. Alfred works full time for a private company testing pesticides, and recently began a second job as a security guard to cover family expenses.

I grew up in a nice neighborhood, but my parents were not really able to afford the lifestyle that most of the people around us did. So I always felt our family was set off because of this. Also, my father is Jewish, and my mother was a Catholic, so I never quite knew what I was and always felt different than either my Christian friends or my Jewish friends. I did go to an orthodox Temple for three years of Hebrew school until I realized that I could never be fully Jewish because of my mother. This was the start of my disenchantment.

At home racism wasn't allowed. My parents were typical progressive, liberal, white Berkeley people. My father always told us how he had once been engaged to a black woman as a young man, and when I asked what happened, he would calmly reply that my grandmother (an Eastern European Jew) had had a nervous breakdown. This is basically the difference between my grandparents' generation and mine.

When I first started dating my first black boyfriend, I knew that there would always be a split between myself and all my grandparents still alive. This I've accepted as something sad, but it's never made me feel like I should have chosen my relatives over my love. So I have mixed feeling towards my heritage and Judaism. Culturally, I still feel Jewish and have incorporated a lot into my new family, like celebrating Hanuakkah, making Jewish food, lighting candles for the dead. Dante is growing up with all of this, plus Christian things like Christmas. I feel fine now about passing on these things to my children, but I still have problems with a lot of the religious aspects of Judaism.

When I was 18 and graduated from high school, Alfred and I got an apartment together. After two years, I started community college and Alfred joined the Army

for three years. This was very hard on both of us, but also good because we had been together with no breaks since I was 17, and now I was alone and he was too. I went through different phases during the three years. At first I was depressed and lonely, then my social life started filling the void and college became something positive to put my energy into. Alfred and I wrote to each other a lot, which was great. For four months I lived with him in a trailer park in Tennessee before he got orders to go to Korea. If he had received orders to go anywhere but Korea, I would have gone! Instead, I transferred to another college and eventually got my degree when I was four months pregnant with Dante.

At present I'm a mother and a wife and eventually would like to become a reading specialist for children. I'm waiting until our daughter Charlotte's old enough, and then it's back to school for me!

There's a kind of paradox for me when it comes to our being an interracial family. On the one hand, I don't think of us as interracial on a conscious level. I don't see myself as white, Alfred black, and the babies brown. Rather, I just see us as us. On the other hand, I am constantly receiving feedback from society at large that is always getting me ready for some conflict over the fact that we are interracial. So it is a strange coexistence within me. I have found that since we had Dante two and a half years ago, I have really felt the importance of having Dante grow up among both black and white children and hopefully around interracial children as well. This has a very large influence on which preschool we chose to involve him in. Luckily, we found one that is very multiethnic. Being with Alfred seems so natural to me. This is how it's been since I was 17 and he was 19. We grew up from kids together.

All in all, I feel proud of the family Alfred and I have made and are making. I'm proud of all the diversity of race and culture involved. Most importantly, I hope our children feel loved enough or confident enough to be individuals making individual choices in life, rather that just going with what's easy or going with the crowd.

Michele Williams

I married when I was 26, and we started our family four years ago in 1988. Michele and I met in high school. We've known each other fifteen years and have been together twelve. We have a family of four and my income is the only income. I am working about fifty hours a week. It's pretty hard because there

Michele, 28, and Alfred Williams, 30, and their son, Dante, 2, and daughter, Charlotte, two weeks old. (1991)

"I feel proud of the family Alfred and I have made and are making. I'm proud of all the diversity of race and culture involved."

— *Michele Williams*

are a lot of medical bills, insurance costs, rent, food, and other costs to keep up with. It's difficult sustaining and enduring, but I figure the longer you endure the better it is. It's hard to know if we're actually doing the right thing, but it's better to do those things and hope that it works out rather than not to do them and pay the price for it.

Shelly and I have hopes that we will be good parents, which means that we learn from our parents' mistakes and not bring them on to our kids. I want my kids to have the things that I never had, like proper education and having two parents in the household, so they won't have to teach themselves and go through life the hard way. I had to teach myself discipline growing up, the discipline of holding on to things I value most and not to give up when things are really hard. It's helped me a lot and brought me to the point that I'm at now. I've never been an individual who's been content with just the minimum. Looking back at how I grew up, my expectations have always been high.

My father left when I was 9 years old, and my mother died when I was about 16. So I basically raised myself with older grandparents. Then my grandmother also passed away, and it was pretty hard growing up. I didn't get to be a kid for very long. I really wouldn't want my children to have to go through losing their parents and not having any proper guidance. My grandparents took over when my mom died. When your grandparents have eighteen grandchildren and all of them are basically living in the same house, it's hard to have any control over all of them. We were left out running around, playing a lot, just being kids. We never went hungry, but we never had much. As young kids we were in the Muslim school with a lot of discipline going on. That was when I was 10 and 11 years old, and I had to go through a lot of changes because I wanted to go to the public school. It's hard to believe that I'm with Michele today because being a Muslim means you don't date outside of your religion. It goes to show you how time changes people.

Being the parents of interracial children, the only thing you can tell your kids is that they are receiving the best from both of you and that they're going to have some racial encountering but they've got to be strong and endure and accept the fact that they are who they are and not worry about everyone else. I fear for them, but I think they'll be strong enough to handle the racism. I'd like my son and daughter to understand how important it is to try to be good, how to be happy, and to stay focused. It's very important to be focused and to stay strong. My children are just naturally smart. I hope that they go to college and become teachers themselves.

I feel that each individual should know that having a family helps direct you. That's your guiding tool. Having kids will mature you a whole lot. It will allow you to look back into your past and see yourself. It will give you the opportunity to become more responsible, more understanding, especially when you have to support your own. You start learning the values of how to manage your money, your time. We're not perfect as parents, but we learn from our mistakes, and we try to rectify them. The thing I have to say to young men nowadays is, get a foot in the door. The main thing is get the education and get your foundation set and start from there.

It's hard for me to spend time with my family, but the little time I do have I spend as much as possible with them. You have to take them camping and fishing and spend that time with them. Kids never forget the things that are most important to them. You can spend all your money on them, and they won't remember that, but the time that you do spend with them they remember.

I want people to know that there are people out there like myself who have been struggling, who are still struggling, who are also in interracial marriages. I have to live for me. I can't live for what people think of me. I can't live their lives for them. I don't criticize anybody for being who they are and doing what they're going to do, as long as they're happy doing it. I try to walk around with my head up and show positiveness and not be on a negative kick. I feel good about myself, I feel strong and healthy. A lot of friends I grew up with never learned the art of holding on, and they've lost so much, like good jobs, and they wonder how I've managed to get to the point where I'm at now. I see it as hard work and endurance and hanging in there with self respect and doing what I had to do to keep abreast of things. I do it because I love my family, and I try to do the things that my father didn't do. I don't want to see my kids having to be hungry, I don't want to see my kids having to struggle, so I endure.

My mother's death really took a toll on me. I think and feel that I was probably closer to my mother than the rest of the kids. I was the only one who really looked like her, the only short one like her. I have memories of times when we were poor, and I had to get out and work hard as a young kid to help support and bring food to the house. Those were good days, just being able to do things like that. I was about 12. I used to work at the grocery store helping people

carry bags to their cars, and I'd work all day until I'd make about $15, and then I'd bring some groceries home, and that really made me feel good. It hasn't been an easy road for me.

The memories I have of my father are very short. I remember him cutting my hair bald, and me getting mad at him for it, and him telling me that I would be able to cut his hair, and I never did. I have a memory of him hopping into his vehicle with his friend and never seeing him again. I never saw him after I was 9 years old, and I don't even know if he's alive. I am just now bringing those issues up about "why." I've even contemplated going through the Red Cross to find him, but I figure if I did that it would bring up bad memories, and I don't know if it would help or if it would hurt more.

I think being in a multiracial marriage is great. I see Michele as being an individual, I don't look at her as just being white or Jewish. I just look at her as being Michele. We were raised in the same area, we went to the same school, we had fun together. There's a lot of things she doesn't like about her own race, and vice versa. Remember, we're just people. And when you're just people you just kind of block out color and you look at individuals. I could care less what people think about me, I got over that a long time ago. Having raised myself, I didn't have time to worry about what someone else thought of me. I feel like this is my life, and we only have one, so enjoy it. No one else is going to do anything for me, I'm going to have to do it for myself.

Michele has always been there for me and I've always been there for her. Occasionally I may get a little static from people and friends who try not to let it out, but they say things like,"Why are you with a white girl?" And I say,"OK, imagine this: are you going to do for me? Are you going to endure for me? Are you going to be there when I'm down? Are you going to love me? No, you're not. So that answers the question." My family loves her, and she's great to them. The guys love her; the girl cousins were skeptical until they met with her. Her family loves me, and I feel accepted by them. I've had my encounters with them too, but I've managed to deal with them and straighten out the problems over the years.

Alfred Williams

Richard Emmons and Barbara Voorhees-Emmons raised seven children, both adopted and biological. After having four biological children — Christopher, Anna, Esther, and Stephen — they adopted Mari from Vietnam when she was 4, and Maria and Toki from Korea when they were 5 and 4. Barbara is a homemaker, refugee resettlement worker and nurse, and Richard is a physician. They consider their Quaker beliefs to be the foundation of their family.

There certainly is growth and change as I look at the photographs taken over the years, yet we haven't really changed all that much. As for my feelings about family, it's very hard to settle on some one thing to put into writing. I think that the enjoyment of life *is* fulfillment of life. I see family and life as interchangeable terms, and if you interlock the members of a family, you have a loving life. I would extend that feeling by adding one of my favorite quotes from Tolstoy:

You must love life
For life is God
And to love life
Is to love God.

I don't think that we set out to have a large family, but you gain experience, see a need, and work with it. We seemed to have the tools for this job. In the process of raising our four biological children, we acquired the space and the interest to add on. Dick's career was such that we could afford the costs, and both his and my training made us feel able to deal with any medical problems that might arise. It just seemed a good cause to which to commit our lives. We decided to adopt children from other backgrounds in order to meet the needs of the children born in wartime—"our wars." They are so innocent and helpless. This was a way we could help with an immediate, existing problem and maybe also improve and help make a better future for us all.

The word "multicultural" comes up often regarding our family or similar families, but in fact we are not multicultural. Our adopted children came to us very young from their countries of birth and early background. They have basically been raised as Americans and will have to learn, as adults, about their biological heritage, culture, and original language. Within the family, we have dealt with their visual differences as marks of beauty, desirable individuality, and valued distinctiveness. We have tried to raise our family as a single unit — attempting to achieve honesty, integrity, and human decency for them all. Our historical Quaker background, on both sides of our families, has given us a solid foundation for our own family structure. We depend daily on this foundation. If anything, we are a Quaker family, not multiracial or adoptive. Adopting was not a new idea for us, since I have several multiracial cousins. I think the word "adoption" has always had and continues to have a positive tone within our family.

The most difficult aspect of raising both biological and adopted children in the same family is countering the deep worry of the adopted children that they are not loved as much as the biological ones are. I think it is safe to say that even the earliest rejection is felt by an infant. Our adopted children were all 4 or 5 years old when they came to us, and by that time had suffered losses many times through no fault of their own. These feelings of insecurity last a long time and are hard to overcome. It is a continuous job of affirmation of love by the parents and family to overcome this.

Another difficulty can be the expenses of raising and educating a large family. Money is a major consideration. However, the greatest joys of a large family are in the diversity of ideas and activities that each member contributes and the security of mutual support and loyalty that the many members provide to each other.

Barbara Voorhees-Emmons

We are all kind of shy about discussing ourselves, especially if it were to be published in a book. My main comment would be that the most significant change is how much we've all grown and matured— and we have added a daughter-in-law, a son-in-law, and a grandson. We are scattered across the U.S. from Boston to Ohio to Indiana to California but still are close-knit, interdependent, and together as often as we can manage.

Richard Emmons

Our family is unique in its variety of cultures and colors meshed together. We admire and uphold traditions going as far back as five generations. Attending Olney Friends School in Barnesville, Ohio, is an example of complete family involvement and commitment to tradition.

The best thing about our family is that we all make extreme efforts to come together for vacations, holidays, special occasions. We love to be together, especially at our mountain cabin. The only thing I wish were different would be that we all lived closer together. Right now we are spread from California to Boston.

Anna Emmons Kirk

Most people tend to think of our family as multicultural; however, in reality, I don't feel as if I carry that sense of deep Vietnamese cultural identity with me. Because of the adoption at such an early period of my life, my social and cultural identity is not Vietnamese; it has been primarily a white, American experience. Because of that, I don't feel like I particularly stand out or am different in any way compared to my siblings and peers. I don't feel that being an adopted Vietnamese child has been an issue in being an equal and full member of this family.

Being disabled by polio, I have been exceptionally lucky to have had the kind of support and encouragement I've had from this family, and they have been truly empowering for me.

Mari Emmons

Richard W. Emmons, 46, and Barbara Voorhees-Emmons, 44, and their children, Christopher, 17, Anna, 15, Esther, 13, Stephen, 10, Mari, 7, Maria, 6, and Toki, 4 years old. (1977)

Richard W. Emmons, Barbara Voorhees-Emmons, Christopher and his wife, Leslie, and their son, Stephen, Anna and her husband, Nathan Kirk, Esther, Stephen, Mari, Maria, and Toki. (1989)

Chiem Kuang Fong and Muey Seng Chao are married and have one biological son, Cheo Kuang Saechao. They immigrated to the United States from Laos in 1980 by way of a refugee camp in Thailand, bringing their son, Cheo Kuang, and Muey Seng's mother, Kaecho Saenang. Once they were settled in the U.S., they adopted a boy, San Ching, from Thailand, and a girl, Mounyk, who is the biological child of Muey Seng's cousin. The following statement was taken from a recorded interview with Muey Seng Chao in 1991.

My husband and I were born in Laos. We came to Thailand to the refugee camp where we met and married. We lived there for five years and our son, Cheo Kuang, was born in Thailand. We came to the United States in 1980 when Cheo Kuang was a baby.

In Laos we can do in our home and we can do in the fields—we can plant rice, everything for ourselves. Here [in the U.S.], we like it. We have a lot of good friends, but it is hard for us because we didn't have no school before. In Laos we didn't have no school, and it's hard for us to learn English and write. We went to adult school for two years, and we learn in the training program. We learn sewing, and we learn how to do a job and how to get a job. Now my husband works in a carpenter shop and I work in the Laotian Handcraft Center on Saturdays, and on weekdays I work as a lab assistant for the California Department of Public Health.

When we came here, we wanted more children, but we couldn't have them. We adopted our little girl, Mounyk, in 1987. She is my cousin. Her parents saw that I have only one child and they have seven. They were just pregnant when they asked me, and I said yes. The boy I adopted, San Ching, is from Thailand. I told my brother [who lives in Thailand] to help me adopt. He found me a little boy whose parents were too poor to keep him. My uncle brought San Ching here from Thailand when he was about 3 years old.

My mother came with us from Thailand. She doesn't speak English. She stays home and my daughter stays home with her. My father died. He was a soldier in Laos, and he died during the fighting there in 1972. I like my life, but hard for me here because I had no school before now. I cannot speak very good English. I cannot write.

Muey Seng Chao

Chiem Kuang Fong, 44, Muey Seng Chao, 33, their children, Cheo Kuang Saechao, 11, San Ching Saefong, 5, Mounyk Kuang Saechao, 3, and Muey's mother, Kaecho Saenang, 72. (1990)

Gabie Berliner became a single parent at 50 years of age when she adopted Daniel at birth. She recently moved in with her mother, Hildegard Berliner, with whom she and Daniel share the home in which Gabie grew up. Hildegard is a psychologist and psychotherapist and Gabie is a clinical social worker and psychotherapist. In the background of the family photograph, a portrait of Hildegard's mother hangs on the wall.

In 1985, when some of my peers were beginning to become grandparents and after a long independent single life, I became a parent by adopting a newborn. I was just 50 when Daniel was born and I adopted him, coincidently, the same age my father was when I was born. I was very lucky as an older single woman to get Daniel as quickly as I did. I went through the same procedure as couples do who adopt via a private attorney—sending out hundreds of letters with a photo to obstetricians, clinics, etcetera, around the U.S. That led to nothing but disappointment. Daniel's birth mother was referred to my attorney, and the staff in his office thought it was a good match. It took only six months from my initial appointment with the attorney until I met his birth mother—a total of one and a half years from when I decided to adopt until he was born. My good health and youthfulness were important in counteracting my age.

It's hard to say what made me realize it was OK to adopt as a single mother. In part it was my slow maturation and tendency to be slow to change and accept changes. In part it has been the more open acceptance by society. It was my therapeutic work with a particular 3-year-old child who became adoptable that inspired me and made me decide. The social worker was considering an older single woman as a candidate to adopt this child, so I thought, "Why not me?"

Now I am making a new, bigger, harder adjusment. Daniel and I have just moved in with my mother in the big house with the big backyard on the flat street where I grew up. In some ways it was hard to leave my little house on a hill. Daniel misses the large room he had there, but there was no place else for him to play, nor children to play with. The hardest part was giving up my autonomy, which I struggled so long to attain. It has been very difficult for Daniel to adjust to two "parents" and having to compete for attention. But my mother and I are working hard at changing our ways, becoming more sensitive and tolerant. Most important, we are working at clarifying our roles so there is more support and less feeling of interference. Daniel seems to be more relaxed and better adjusted, clearer about rules and expectations, less defiant because my mother and I get along better. And, of course, there are advantages to our new arrangement. My mother spends lots of time with Daniel and is a great help and support. Our shared housekeeper has only one household to deal with. Best of all, I don't have to schlepp Daniel and his baggage back and forth every time my mother babysits!

Gabie Berliner, 54, her son Daniel, 4, and Hildegard Berliner, 82, Gabie's mother. (1989)

> *"The greatest gifts Daniel's grandmother offers? He gains a perspective of older people, their needs and limitations, their wisdom and experience. He gets family history and tradition."*
>
> — *Gabie Berliner*

The greatest gifts Daniel's grandmother offers? He gains a perspective of older people, their needs and limitations, their wisdom and experience. He gets family history and tradition. Daniel also has another adult family member to do special things with and for him (she has endless energy). I hope Daniel develops a respect and compassion for older people from the example of my caring for my mother—the way I did from watching my mother caring for her parents.

I grew up in a semitraditional family. It was "traditional" only in the respect of having both a mother and father. But my father was considerably older, although I never thought of him as old. We did a lot of things together, especially on vacation, but he was emotionally remote, which made my relationship with my mother more intense. My half siblings were older and on their own, so I grew up as an only child. Even now I would like another child, in part so my son grows up with a sibling to share the joys and burdens he'll experience in his family. It would be especially good for him to have a brother. He is surrounded by females, including our wonderful babysitter-housekeeper. When Daniel is with us he thinks being a girl is better. At nursery school he plays with the boys in the usual rough-and-tumble play they do.

My hopes for Daniel are that he will grow up to be a happy, well-adjusted person; that he will have self-confidence, strivings, and can make choices in his life that bring him pleasure and success; and that he will have good skills to cope with difficult times. I see my role as providing him with security and stability without being judgmental or restrictive in my expectations. I want him to learn that it's OK to be different, think differently, feel differently than his mother. That was difficult for me to experience as a child. I also want to model the values I acquired and cherish: honesty, caring about his fellow beings and nature, using nonviolent ways of solving problems.

What would I change if I were to start over? I wish only that I had come to the point of knowing that it was right for me to have a baby as a single parent at a much younger age. That is, if I hadn't met and married the right man and had children naturally, which was always my dream and expectation. But I am lucky to have inherited a youthful physical make-up and to have youthful attitudes and personality. I am proud of my son and hope that he will never have cause to feel embarrassed or regretful that he is adopted or has an "older" mother-only parent.

Gabie Berliner

I grew up in a traditional European family, the oldest and only girl with three younger brothers; two of them were much younger than I. I loved and idealized both my parents and feared them a little. I adored my brothers. In my generation and small-town environment, women didn't count for much, except my mother—she was special. In order to identify (and to outdo her) I had to become not only a supermom but also find a useful place in the world. Finding a man who could compare with my father wasn't easy. I found one old enough to almost be my father. We were married for forty-three years. Gabie remained our only child. I had to find all kinds of ways to become "supermom" and make a place for myself. When my husband died thirteen years ago, I did have an extended family and a profession, but being alone had to be learned. Then followed a brief interlude with a partner who soon became ill and died in my arms. Again I was alone. By this time there was Daniel!

From birth, Daniel seemed to me like a reincarnation of his mother and a wonder to behold. I cherished sharing in his care and observing his development, strenuous as it became, as I was nearing and passing 80 years old. It meant rushing from place to place for all of us and some instability for Daniel. When Gabie brought up the idea of living together, I soon knew how fulfilling it would be. We also recognized the risks. How would we resolve inevitable problems and frictions? How would we assure autonomy? Would we be able to not inflict our conflicts on Daniel? Even though we have a great deal of respect for each other, how can we minimize hurting each other's feelings? Or avoid it altogether? Even though we share basic views about child rearing, our different temperaments and stages in the life cycle produce different ways of handling the day-to-day exigencies of Daniel's needs, wishes, behaviors. There can only be one mother. How will I fit in?

None of these questions has been answered once and for all. We work on the answers. There is laughter and there are tears; there is much love and cooperation, and there is tension and anger. I am now 84 years old (and look shriveled and ancient). Being around high-energy Daniel is wonderful and exhausting. To witness and partake of his inexhaustible enthusiasm for all aspects of life takes the sting out of the expectation of death. His celebration of life contributes greatly to making mine worthwhile. Since my only fear of life in old age is a fear of stagnation, I also cherish my work as a psychotherapist. It feels good to be useful in this special way.

When Daniel was born, I saw in him that same exquisite capacity to make his needs known through the gentlest messages that I had seen in Gabie and very soon to respond to the world with the same kind of sensitivity. Later the similarities revealed themselves in a rare combination of colorfully rich imagination, fantasy, and humor, with a vivid interest in the realities of life. These are all characteristics which I loved in my husband, Gabie's father. It is precious to see them develop in our little boy. Lately, however, he is also developing in other directions. He is becoming much more aggressive, especially verbally, than Gabie (or her father) ever were.

Our life together is never quite free of tensions, but to me it feels as if we are quite successful in dealing with them (partially by having it out and partially by learning to let go). There are sacrifices for everybody, but on balance, I feel we all benefit. Our hope is that our little boy will draw from this family constellation a firm sense of identity, the knowledge that he is loved, a solid sense of values, and a joy of life. The rest will be up to him. I hope that I will have the privilege to see him grow at least into middle boyhood and that I can assist my daughter with the great task she has chosen.

Hildegard Berliner

I love my mom more than my guns. I love my blanket and my mom the same. I wish I had a dog or a pet panda. I wish I had a brother or sister. I wish I was always a baby but the only thing that was missing would be my guns.

I love my family.

Daniel Berliner

Denise and Neil Jacobson, both of whom have cerebral palsy, adopted David when he was a newborn. At first, it was believed David also had cerebral palsy; however, David has no physical disability. Denise is a writer, and Neil is a computer systems architect.

I had always wanted a baby, but I was never very vocal about it. I didn't want to be thought of as "unrealistic." After all, with my disability, cerebral palsy, just day-to-day living is an experience. Little things that non-disabled people do so quickly, automatically, and effortlessly—putting toothpaste on a toothbrush, pouring coffee, getting dressed—took me time, concentration, and energy. Why choose to make my life more involved and complicated? Then, I met Neil...

Neil, a very logical and independent man—a systems analyst in private industry—also has cerebral palsy, very similar to mine. On our first date he shared with me his dream of adopting a disabled child—a dream he had since he was 5 years old.

Our son, David, was barely six weeks old and all set to be adopted by another couple, until they found out he might have cerebral palsy. Through a sophisticated network, a friend of a friend of ours, both very involved in the Disability Rights Movement, called to find out if Neil and I were interested in adopting the infant. Two months later, when the paperwork cleared, David came home.

Before I saw the baby for the first time, I had fears and doubts that covered everything from "How will Neil and I physically handle this baby?" to "What if this child turns out not to be disabled and climbs trees?" I also had concerns about adoption and bonding. Then I met him. As I held David in my arms for the first time, his blue eyes looked into mine with such magnetic force that I felt as if my heart had been pierced by a finely pointed needle sewing our bond with indelible thread. In my whole life, I'd never felt joy so deeply. I knew that for whatever reason, Neil, David, and I were meant to be a family.

That was over two and a half years ago. David has outgrown those suspicious little quirks that played such a significant role in landing him into our lives. Sometimes I think that David had orchestrated the whole elaborate plan just to get out to California. It's a thrill to wake up each morning and see his smile. It's bliss to hear him say, "Hi, Mommy." I have never before experienced a feeling of such total acceptance and love.

Denise, 39, and Neil Jacobson, 36, and their son, David, 2 years old. (1989)

"Whereas I thought I would be the role model for my son, I quickly learned that it was David who had the lessons for me to learn....he was, and still is, the only person who doesn't care about my having a disability!"

— *Neil Jacobson*

The relationship between Neil and David is one of mutual adoration. David has touched something deep in his dad that allows Neil the freedom of physical affection. Neil was never terribly at ease with hugging and kissing, but with David sitting in his lap watching TV or going for a ride, Neil can't resist giving David a peck on the cheek or a loving squeeze.

For me, raising David is a mixture of humor, frustration, fatigue, challenge, and most of all, love. I wouldn't want it any other way.

Denise Sherer Jacobson

When I was 4 1/2 years old, my doctor recommended to my parents that I be institutionalized. He felt that, due to their traumatic experience being in the Holocaust, they were unable to cope with the severity of my disability. My father visited the institution and came home horrified. He described how most of the children lay on the floor, half naked, starving, shivering and abandoned. My father cried. My parents found the courage to say "No" to the doctor and kept me. It was then that I first began dreaming of someday adopting a child with a disability.

Twelve years later, as a senior in high school, I visited that same institution. I, too, witnessed hungry looks in children, teenagers roaming the halls aimlessly, young adults staring into nothingness. I knew ever so clearly that I would have been and could have been one of them. My desire to adopt grew.

In college I became very involved with the movement for the disabled, organizing rallies, holding sit-ins, lobbying, doing public speaking, etcetera. All the while, I felt that helping "the masses" was one thing, but that the real test, the real challenge would be to help one child see beauty in this world.

At age 34 I got my chance. From the moment Denise described her phone conversation with this stranger from St. Louis, I knew that my life was about to change. When I heard that he was born on my birthday, this chill ran up and down my spine, and I knew that this was meant to be. On March 20, 1987, at 5:50 p.m., as David's foster mother majestically carried him off the plane and delivered him snugly in my lap, my heart stopped. All my dreams, hopes, and anxieties seemed to flash by at that split moment. I looked down, and David's eyes seemed to say "Well, here we go...."

Whereas I thought I would be the role model for my son, I quickly learned that it was David who had the lessons for me to learn. David, for instance, was, and still is, the only person who doesn't care about my having a disability! When David woke up at 2 a.m. and was hungry, he cried! He did not care that I was tired or how hard it might be for me to get out of bed. He wanted his bottle! How wonderful it is to have someone be so clear about their needs. At 4 a.m. when David needed to poop, he pooped! Again, he did not consider the difficulty it may be for me to change him. He just pooped! And he demanded that I clean him! I never realized the joy and sense of wholeness one derives knowing that another human being needs you! When David was older, I was continually amazed that he wanted me to help him even when there were non-disabled friends around who could help him much much faster than I. The reason for this turned out to be quite simple. I'm DADDY!

I love being David's Daddy!

Neil Jacobson

Tony Mello, a single gay man, adopted Paul, who has cerebral palsy, when Paul was 12 years old. Tony also has a biological son, Jon Mello, 20, from a previous marriage, and another adopted son, Michael, 19, who now lives on his own. Tony bought a house with Zana and Tom Rose, a married couple, and they consider themselves "family," sharing all financial and emotional concerns within the household.

My family has changed over the years. My family has changed with my age, my values, beliefs, and with my experiences. Today it seems that I expect less and have so much more. I know today that one does not own nor can control others, though I *still* try at times. I'm learning to judge and condemn less and to accept and love more, and this process must begin with myself. I know myself a little better each day.

My biological son, Jon, has moved on to begin his own new family, and I have done the same. Jon and I know something about freedom to be ourselves, trust, honesty, integrity, faith, inner peace, and serenity. We had twenty years together to experience, and experience we did! Our "relationship," our "family," was tested by unfaithfulness, pretension, disgrace, and much shame. Issues of control and addiction entered into our family. I knew everything twenty-five years ago, and today I know *so* little. I do believe that people need people—and a "family" affords us the opportunity to be together and get some of these needs met.

Jon and his partner, Stacey, and my granddaughter, Ashlyn, are with me in my heart every moment of every day. They give me hope for mankind. Jon, while very much his own person at age 20, is still my son, which simply means I've had twenty remarkable years with another human, and today we share unconditional love for each other. I could ask for no more.

It is difficult writing about my current family and other family issues because these things change from day to day—and they seem difficult for me to make sense of while I am in the middle of them.

One of my adopted sons, Michael, is 18. I adopted him when he was 9 years old. It's been an incredible nine years. The reason that I adopted Michael (and my son Paul) has some significant psychological base—probably mostly self-centered—that I'm unclear about. "I" was never enough. As it turns out, as a single gay male I had a tough go of it adopting a child. My willingness to accept one of society's "throwaway" children increased the chance of success.

I know that I didn't want my children to experience some of the trauma that I had in early childhood. I believed that I had hidden powers—godlike I suppose—whereby I could heal with love any damage done to my children prior to their placement with me. Michael was severely abused as an infant and

Tony Mello, 41, his son, Paul (Scoot) Mello, 18, and "extended family" members Zana and Tom Rose. (1989)

"My family has changed with my age, my values, beliefs, and with my experiences. Today it seems that I expect less and have so much more."

— *Tony Mello*

then routinely neglected by the county placement office. To this day he suffers from early deprivation. He's been treated with toxic medications for all of his years and has spent most of his 18 years institutionalized. The adoption was clearly a mistake. I didn't adopt a child to have him grow up in mental institutions. I accept my role (as he and I define it) as his father today. Our contact is limited to a visit six or eight times a year and a phone call once a month. I am aware that I'm the only consistent significant person in his life and that I am powerless to make things better for him. He lives in a boarding-type situation collecting social security income. I am afraid for him.

On the other hand, my son Paul is a success story. I adopted Paul when he was 12 years old. Considered another one of society's throwaway children, Paul has cerebral palsy and is mildly retarded; however, he functions quite well and requires little assistance. Paul is personable and loving, independent, rewarding. He has helped to put balance in my life. He is like a barometer of the energy in the family. Paul is a teacher—I feel that I was blessed to get him. The Department of Social Services has no idea how wonderful Paul is—if they did, they might have selected a straight, two-parent family for him.

I've started a new family with Tom and Zana. Last year they had been looking to leave the company we all three worked for and move to a rural area. I had the same plans, so we shared our ideas. I had always been drawn to this Northern California coastal area, and they fell in love with it, so we decided to do it together. They adore Paul. We lived together in a smaller home for several months before buying this home together. We learned to adjust to each other's small idiosyncracies. We share one bank account as well as our vehicles, the mortgage on our home, and the care and parenting of my son Paul. There is much relief in knowing one doesn't have all the adult responsibility. I treasure this. And one day we may share unconditional love. Obviously we have trust and each other's well-being at heart. Paul is disabled and I am different in that I am a gay man. Tom and Zana are special in their own ways too. We live in a very small coastal village, and acceptance plays a major role in the bonding of this family—in the home and in the town.

The three of us, for example, were instrumental in providing wheelchair access for Paul at home and making a decision to spend substantial money to remodel our home to meet his needs—and to lobby in the community for access and at his high school for special requirement needs.

With just a little encouragement from his family, Paul has been able to articulate his needs to his school district to raise and lower tabletops, to provide rails in bathrooms, make doorways accessible, and purchase a new van equipped with a wheelchair lift. Paul can and is meeting goals of his own regularly.

Tony Mello

There is so much I could say about our new family—the motivation, the implementation, the goals. It's really very complex, like all other families, and hard to condense. We are basically trying to provide ourselves with a quality of life that promotes personal growth while remaining economically sound. This arrangement brings four incomes to the home and allows us to work toward financial security. It is a constant balancing act. We are committed to the wellness of each family member. Each of the four of us has very distinct needs. Trust and acceptance of difference is at the core. The physical, emotional, intellectual, and spiritual needs of each individual are important to all. Because it is planned, the family functions at a high level with a general feeling of optimism and well-being. All mundane chores are done with joy or are not done until the attitude is good. We do lots of things together but respect an individual's need to be alone.

This is probably not a lifelong arrangement. At this time we are in a period of great change and growth, and we will reach a point where the growing will demand a change in the arrangement. When that time comes, we will feel good about our life in the family. The ties will be there forever, but we will simply move on.

Zana Rose

Tom and Zana make me feel better than ever before. Tom takes me for rides in his trucks . . . and I like Zana's antiques. We get to have lots of pizza.

Some of my old families abused me . . . before my dad adopted me. They burned me with cigarettes and slapped me around, and sometimes they didn't let me eat. They just punished me for no reason. They put me to bed early for no reason. I was unhappy.

This family is peaceful and not at all like the old families. I like it here better than there, and I get to go places now. I used to have to share a room, and now I have my own room and my own bathroom. I was unhappy. Now I'm happy. I can go to the park whenever I want. People here are nicer.

Paul (Scoot) Mello

Patrice Harrison-Inglis is the primary wage earner, working as an executive secretary, and Larry Harrison-Inglis, a Vietnam veteran, is the homemaker. Their lives changed dramatically when their son, Ben, was first diagnosed with leukemia when he was 18 months old. Ben has since recovered and he and his brother, Les, and their parents live in their mountain home.

Our current situation is something that just grew out of our circumstances—it isn't something we really decided. My happiness seems to depend on making changes to match things that happen. That's never my first reaction—I always try to dig in—but Larry is ready and able to let go of things that at first seem essential. I am so glad because things have NOT gone predictably for us.

At the start of our marriage we had our two incomes, a house with a mortgage, and all of that. I was at home for the end of my first pregnancy and for Ben's first nine months. When I returned to full-time work from 8 to 5 each day, Larry switched his work to the evening shift and we had Ben with a babysitter for just two or three hours a day.

Everything changed dramatically when Ben was diagnosed, at 18 months, with one of the rarer and deadliest forms of leukemia. Suddenly my naturally-birthed, still breastfeeding, beautiful boy required everything a big high-tech hospital could give him—most of it painful and frightening. The very morning they told us what the tests were for, I called my office and told them they wouldn't be seeing me for a while. When we had digested the diagnosis and heard the treatment plan, I let my employer know that I would be occupied for a full 14 months. Everything other than Ben's survival become so minor! Larry's instincts were to lighten our responsibilities everywhere else. This was tragic for me at first, but soon felt like a relief. The yard sale we held as the house entered foreclosure felt like a magic sacrifice: everything from my good work clothes to the kitchen pots and pans were sold or given away. In exchange, I hoped Ben would somehow survive against the dismal odds the doctors gave us.

During that year we were in the hospital for more than three weeks out of every four. Between my fears for my own baby and getting to know the other families of children on that cancer ward, we were immersed in the "one-day-at-a-time" philosophy—and this has not entirely left us, even yet. Larry kept working and slept in a little borrowed trailer in the hospital parking lot while I kept my cot next to the hospital bed, and we cooked meals in the unit's day room. We watched most of the other families struggle to maintain their normal lifestyles and thought they suffered more for it.

Patrice, 36, and Larry Harrison-Inglis, 44, and their sons, Ben, 10, and Les, 7. (1991)

"...this arrangement of ours seems like the best of two worlds: Momma home with the babies and Daddy home with "big boys."

— *Patrice Harrison-Inglis*

Larry and I promised each other we would not return to our "upwardly mobile", two-income way of life as long as we had a child to care for. That way of living now seems like such a rat race! My heart aches for friends at work whose husbands and wives are also career people ... their children (even new infants!) in daycare for these long days.

Ben not only survived his year of intensive chemotherapy without permanent side effects, he remained a sweet-natured, happy, and outgoing boy. We felt incredibly lucky. There were absolutely no assurances given about his future health, but we knew not to ask for those. What else was possible except to go forward with optimism? Les was born the year after our ordeal. So there were four of us when Ben experienced a relapse at age five. With all our unasked-for expertise about childhood cancer, the second diagnosis was ten times as fearful as the first had been. We knew his chances were terribly diminished.

We closed up our little cabin, friends accepted our pets, we left the garden to wither, and the four of us lived between the hospital and the nearby home of a dear friend for more than a year. We tried to treat the whole thing as an adventure. Things happened to all of us together; neither Larry nor I was left to hold it all together—we let "it" fall apart—and I think that was the key to our survival. Ben has now passed the five year mark of his second recovery. He eats as much as his daddy at dinner and gets fewer winter colds than any of us!

For a little while, both Larry and I were at home with the boys and only did odd jobs. Our idea was to take turns as the wage earner, and we resigned ourselves to living very cheaply while raising our children. Larry has been a medical worker (nursing and X-ray technology), and I have done office work. As far as income level, these two sorts of work were interchangeable, and both seemed to allow for relatively easy entry (and exit!) from the job market. As it happens though, I find myself very well placed as an executive secretary and my salary would be hard to duplicate by an "entry" for Larry now.

The contrast between our rented mountain property (with our chickens, milk goats and big vegetable garden) and my high-tech office is fun—work days go by very quickly, weekends like lightening! Now that we are in the midst of it, this arrangement of ours seems like the best of two worlds: Momma home with the babies and Daddy home now with "big boys." Unless we were to have another child, I'll be happy to keep working ... to have Larry home with a new baby would feel like a real sacrifice to me. I don't feel attached to my career—it supports us; I might find a real vocation later. Lately I feel really well supported by Larry at home—it leaves me time and energy to spare and keeps me from feeling ordinary!

Patrice Harrison-Inglis

People ask me, "What do you do?" and I have to think twice before I answer. When we were leasing the orchard, I would just say, "I'm a farmer." On this past year's tax return, Patrice wrote her occupation as secretary and mine as homemaker. So what do I do? I built this house; I work on the eleven acres around our place and the owner's house, who lives nearby—this keeps our rent low. With a fire five years ago, the drought, and then the big earthquake last year, we have lost a lot of big trees. So there is woodcutting and clearing of brush and erosion control work more or less constantly. I maintain the water system for the two households and work on our vehicles and other equipment.

I roust the boys out of bed and get them ready to go on weekdays with breakfast and packed lunches and drive them to school. I either pick them up or meet the bus, depending upon the other "chauffeur" duties (to violin or art lessons) that day. While they're gone, I do the laundry, clean up the house, feed the chickens, split firewood, that sort of thing. After school I like to get Ben and Les involved in outdoor work if I can—plumbing, working on the cars or the farm vehicles. Patrice does the cooking, but I do all the grocery shopping and hauling in other supplies, like hay for her goats. I volunteered in the remedial reading program at the school for a couple of years and in Les' kindergarten class. Once in a while I still do volunteer work at Children's Hospital. What else? I have a health club membership; I hardly ever miss a baseball, basketball or football game on the radio. I love it; I feel spoiled, really. I do all these things on my own schedule.

Larry Harrison-Inglis

When Daddy used to pick me up, before the earthquake [in 1989], at the other school, he was practically the only Dad and all the others were Moms waiting at the fence. I liked that because Dad knows everybody and the teacher too. Now kids say after class, "Ask your Mom if you can come over." Instead I ask my Dad. It surprises them.

It's fun when Daddy goes on the school field trips. When we get home from school on regular days, Daddy is usually working outside. Maybe some other guys are here building something or cutting down the big trees. When they had the sawmill set up in the meadow, I would go up there and do my homework. Even though it was really noisy, it was fun! Also, when he was in charge of the orchard and there were people working with him pruning or picking, we helped and were learning to speak Spanish. I think it's interesting to have Dad work at home.

I like it when Momma works downtown. She can get things from the store on her way home; also if I need pencils or xerox copies of my reports and things. In the summer, Dad and Les and I go down and have lunch with her, and she is wearing a dress and high heels and has make-up on. After we eat, sometimes we can go inside her office and see the goldfish. Once in a while, we stay there while she works and play with the computers, high-lighter pens and the copy machine!

Ben Harrison-Inglis

It's nice having Daddy home. I kind of wish *both* of them could be home all the time. Most Moms and Dads go to work and the kids go to babysitters all by themselves. Once, when Daddy worked at the mechanic shop, I went to the babysitters's when I was littler and I just wanted to go to work with Daddy instead. At babysitters' they don't have remote-control cars and my bike like I do at home, so I'm lucky.

Les Harrison-Inglis

Franz Baumhackl was divorced in 1973 and shared custody of the children, Mitja Che and Aaron, with their mother. The boys lived with Franz for two years because their mother had remarried and was living in a distant city. Rephotographed in 1989, Franz Baumhackl had recently married Tim, whom he met in Thailand. Franz is a graphic designer, Aaron works in a restaurant and hopes to start his own business, and Mitja Che works as a secretary while on leave from school and spends his spare time fighting for civil liberties.

It has been approximately thirteen years since Helen Nestor took a photo of me, my brother, and my father. I am now 22 years old and, looking back at my childhood, it is quite evident that my parents should not have had kids with each other. We are all still on speaking terms—remarkable, since the past years got pretty rough.

When my mom and dad got divorced, I was about 4 years old and my brother, Aaron, was almost 2. The judge issued a ruling of joint custody with the condition that my brother and I remain together. I am very thankful for this condition. I am closer to my brother than to either of my parents because he was with me in my two households.

Except for a period of two years when my mom lived in San Diego, my brother and I switched houses every week. On paper, this might sound like a reasonable interpretation of joint custody, but, in reality, it made for a schizophrenic childhood. My parents each ran their household in a radically different manner. My mom served a nearly vegetarian dinner every night promptly at 5:30 p.m. while my dad ate a lot of fried foods with a lot of meat around 9 p.m. My mom always set curfews. My dad set none. My dad wouldn't wake up on weekends until noon, while my mom woke my brother and me by 9 a.m. I wouldn't say that one house was "better" than the other, but I hated having to move between the two. I never quite unpacked in one house before having to move to the other, and my homework or favorite article of clothing always seemed to be left behind at the other house. I believe that although I stayed at my "mom's house" or "my dad's house," I never really considered either place to be home. My brother was a sort of continuing thread between the two houses.

My memory is a little fuzzy, but I remember my mom living with my stepfather almost immediately after my parents separated. At 22 I can look back and see that my stepfather may have had good intentions, but he failed miserably as my stepfather. From the age of 5 until I moved out from my mom's house at 14, my stepfather was only a terror in my life. He was very possessive: there was his TV chair, his workspace corner of the living room, his personal towel, his special fork, his cooking knives and Teflon pans, his stereo. And the rules were not to be broken. I recollect actually being hit three times, but the constant threats, chases around the house, and raised fists were much more intimidating. My mom repeatedly sent me to a therapist (actually, about five therapists in total) and each therapist would begin by asking me if I resented my stepfather because he was taking the place of my father. I would always respond, "No, he's an asshole." After a few sessions, my mom would be asked to come, and then my stepfather would be asked to join in as well. And then, every time, I was told by the therapist, "Mitja, you don't need to come in next week; I'd like to meet with your mom and stepfather for a session or two." And that was the end of therapy. After years of threats from someone whose drinking only amplified the meanness already there, I moved out of my mom's house into my dad's apartment. The saying, "Out of the frying pan and into the fire," applies nicely here.

Until I moved in full-time with my dad, we had a pretty good arrangement. My brother and I would eat meals with him and go out sometimes, but the remaining free time my brother and I spent without rules such as curfews or mandatory studying time. My father was dating a lot and was not around very often anyway. By this time, I was in high school and was failing many of my classes. I would skip classes to hang out with friends in cafes. I don't think that this bothered my dad too much, but my mother calling him, concerned about my lack of progress, bugged the hell out of him. My father was also an alcoholic, and our household had a lot of irrational arguments: I have always had a sharp tongue and do not back down from confrontations. My brother, on the other hand, always managed to be the baby of the family and would be lurking somewhere in the background, watching the fireworks and occasionally snickering at the ridiculousness of it all.

I recall going out in the evening and coming home to a drunk father who had been stewing all evening on something simple: he considered my room to be a mess. With alcohol, a messy room sometimes meant that I had left a few books on the floor or hadn't put my laundry away or had piles of paper on my desk. While I'll allow that my room always could have been cleaner, my father's response to the situation was out of line. At least three times I came home to find all of my possessions thrown into garbage bags to be sorted out and "put away properly." All of my possessions: clothes, books, records, computer, letters, photos. Everything. I moved out when the following two things happened: he hit me on two separate occasions, and I once came home to find all of my belongings gone. My brother, alone when I came home one evening, said, "I don't know what you've done, but Franz is pissed, and you'd better get out of here. All of your stuff is with him in the Toyota." My father had threatened before to throw everything of mine off of the local pier, and although I found out later that he didn't actually carry out the threat, I didn't wait around at the time to find out. I called two friends of mine, a wonderful couple in their early 30s, and moved in with them at the age of 15 and stayed with their family for almost three years before renting my own room in another household.

These are things I remember most from my childhood, and it seems that many of the good times have been clouded over by them. Not all was bad, though. I remember camping trips, blowing the paper off of straws at restaurants, bicycling through a local park, and the Beatles' "Here Comes the Sun" playing while cooking fried matzoh on Sunday mornings. My brother and I have stuck together throughout the years. It seems that the best times I remember were preteenage years. Some family traditions still carry on, such as celebrating the holidays together. My brother and I usually spend Christmas Eve with our father, where we decorate the two-foot-tall living tree, and then the next morning head over to our mom's house for breakfast and more gift-giving. My father has a lot of pictures from my childhood, and looking through them I am reminded that there were many good times.

But to focus on those things, I feel, would be to gloss over a big part of my childhood. I dropped out of high school (with no real regrets) because I chose to make friends instead of going to classes. I have been told—and this bio probably shows it—that I am extremely cynical. I have shunned almost all financial help from my family as I slowly work my way through college. I have learned not to depend on other people and to listen to my own gut feelings above anyone else's.

Now, in 1991, our family has almost come full circle. I spent the last two years living in New York City, and my brother has just returned from six months in Greece. The two of us now live together in an apartment in the same building our father lives in, which allows us to be with our father, but gives everyone some space. My brother and I often have dinner with our parents, although we both definitely keep a little bit of emotional distance from them. Overall, our "family life" has vastly improved from the way it was a few years ago. Perhaps the most important change has been that my father stopped drinking after I moved out. My brother and I are glad to see him happily remarried. I don't think that either of my parents were ready to have kids when they did. Now, on my mom's side, I have a 5-year-old baby brother (half-brother), and I'm not quite sure what to expect from my father and his wife in the next few years. After my brother and me, I think that my mom and dad are a lot more prepared for parenthood, and I believe that the next ten years will be much better.

Mitja Che Baumhackl

*Franz Baumhackl, 33, and
his sons Mitja Che, 9, and
Aaron, 7 years old. (1978)*

Franz Baumhackl, 46, his
new wife, Tim Baumhackl,
24, and his grown sons Mitja
Che, (left) 22, and Aaron, 20.
(1991)

Billye and Ivory Carson have adopted five children as well as raising Billye's two sons by previous marriages. Ivory is a welder and Billye is a homemaker and nurse. Aysheia and Yvette are college students. The Carsons describe themselves as "natural, foster, adoptive, and legal guardian parents."

First, I would like to go back and bring you up to date on how all of this came to be. It started back on March 7, 1975, when I met Ivory. Being divorced, I had come up against many problems, especially at parties, where a divorced woman tends to get hassled by men. So rather than go through that, I would always find a nice gentleman to escort me to and from the parties. So on this particular night my girlfriend recommended a friend of her husband, Ivory, as a possible escort. For months Ivory remained just an escort when I needed one. Then, after about four months, we started dating each other. I was very cautious because I had two boys by my previous marriages, so I didn't want them exposed to just anybody. During our eleven months of courtship, we talked about many things: us getting married, Ivory adopting my two sons, us adopting a little girl, and my career as a nurse. On February 14, 1976, we were married.

All my life I liked caring for children. I am the seventh child and the only girl out of eight children. As a young girl growing up on a farm in Mississippi, I would always go get someone's baby and keep the baby all day. I loved taking care of babies. When I had two boys of my own, I wanted a girl, but was told that due to medical problems I would probably never have any more children. Ivory had not been previously married nor had any children, so we talked about adopting one. Since we had not been married long, I knew our chances for adopting a baby were slim to none because we did not meet the requirements. I had heard about foster children, so we decided to give it a try because we knew we could give a child love, a family environment, and a home. We were scared to be foster parents because we didn't want to get a child, start loving it, and then have to give the child up. So we talked with a social worker about a child that would possibly be given up for adoption.

After one year of marriage, we received our first foster children. We started out to get one girl, Aysheia, who was 6 years old, but since she had a little eighteen-month-old brother, Kino, in the same foster-care home, we decided to take the two of them. After two years of visits by the mother, who showed no real progress or interest in getting help for herself, the

Billye, 49, and Ivory Carson, 42, and their children, Aysheia Carson, 21, Kino Carson, 15, Curtis Hill, 12, Yvette Martin, 18, and her infant son, William Cherry, Jr., six weeks old. (1991)

children were put up for adoption.. As foster parents, we had the first chance at adoption. That was a happy day for me, for now I would have my daughter and another son. The mother protested, so the trials went back and forth for about three years, and the adoption wasn't final for another two years, which means that after eight years the children legally became Carsons.

I continued working as a Licensed Vocational Nurse (LVN) during the time we had begun proceedings to adopt Aysheia and Kino. Then Aysheia voiced her concern about being an only girl with three brothers, so we discussed it as a family and decided to go for a sister. Little did I know we would be asked within the next few weeks to take this family of three—two boys and a girl. They were brought over to our home on January 1, 1982, for a week trial and get-acquainted visit. They never left or went back to the emergency shelter. I worked as an LVN for two more years and then had to quit for health reasons that had gotten worse over a period of ten years. So on December 31, 1983, I quit work. Now I had time to spend with my five young children. Aysheia had many continual physical and emotional problems, and the others also had severe emotional problems that needed to be taken care of. So that's what I devoted my time and talents to.

In 1981 I, Ivory, and our daughter, Aysheia, accepted Jesus Christ as our personal savior. That's when we started seeing positive changes. Since then, as our family increased, all have accepted Christ as their Savior and Lord. We are not by any means saying that our lives are trouble-free or without problems, but we don't feel hopeless now. Even though it appears that we have more problems now, by the grace of God, we are able to face them and work through them. Now as natural, foster, adoptive, and legal guardian parents, we give all praises to God through Jesus Christ for our children today. To this date we have had to give up only one child who had more emotional problems than we were able to continuously deal with or able to help. We still have four children and the grandchild living with us. One thing we have that no one can take away is our love for each other and our family closeness bond. They all may not be what we wanted them to be nor what they desire to be, but our children are encouraged to be the best that they can be no matter what.

Billye Carson

I am a 42-year-old Christian man and the proud and happy husband of Billye Carson, and proud father of Ronnie, Emmett, Aysheia, Yvette, Kino, and Curtis (Mickey).

Before I met my wife, Billye, I was kind of just drifting with no real purpose or goals in life. Even though I am the oldest child of thirteen children, and we all are very close, my life was still empty. When Billye and I met we agreed to just be casual friends. After four months we began dating, and seven months later we were married.

During the next twelve months we discussed many things. We were very happy and considered ourselves very lucky to have found each other. During this time we found out that we could not have any more children. And even though we had two sons, we wanted a daughter. So we discussed adopting a girl. We found out later that we didn't meet the state's requirements. So we sat down with the two boys and talked about becoming a foster family. The boys were both happy and sad. They had just begun to adjust to having a new daddy around; now we were talking about adding other children. Well, it took a lot of talking and lots of love to assure them that we loved them and no one would or could ever change that or take their place in our hearts and lives. Fourteen months had passed when we got our first two foster children, Aysheia and Kino; by then Ronnie and Emmett were happy to be big brothers. Eight years later Aysheia and Kino were fully adopted.

In 1981, me, Billye and Aysheia invited Jesus to come into our hearts to live, and He did. Before this we had a good life, after we accepted Christ we gained eternal life and learned how to have and live a better life here on earth.

In 1982 we were blessed with three more children, Yvette, Robert, and Curtis (Mickey). Now we have seven. God's word tells us that He *rested* on the seventh day. We *stopped* with the seventh child. Since then we had to give up one of our children. And since God created Heaven and Earth in six days and we ended up with six children, we feel that we are still truly blessed to have them, and our four grandchildren Sharifa, Kenneth, William, and a new grandson, Emmett L. Granville III.

Today I am a very happy man, and I thank God every day for my beautiful wife, Billye, our six children, four grandchildren, four godchildren, our parents, families and Christian friends. Oh, and let me not forget our dog, "One-pound."

Ivory Vonell Carson

When I was first put into a foster home I thought to myself, "Oh, no. I must have been a bad girl and made Mommy mad a me." Even though Mommy explained to me, "Baby, I love you and want you to have all the material things that all little boys and girls have and need. Right now I can't give them to you, so I'll give you to someone who will do the things that I can't, but remember I love you." We say, "OK Mommy, we love you too, and we promise to always love you."

After she leaves us we're placed in our homes and filled with hope that some day the doorbell will ring and it'll be Mommy. Now it's time to adjust to a new family and friends while trying to cope with a new environment. My new foster parents are nice, but they do things that Mommy never did and they have rules that we have to follow. I see now it's going to be hard to adjust to calling a stranger Mama and Daddy, and say, "This is my brother and sister." Well, surprisingly enough, adjusting to a new family was easy, but the kids at school would soon find out and would want to know why this happened to me and where is my real mother and father.

My biggest question then and now is how can a 9-year-old tell others, "My Mommy loved me; that's why she gave me up." You know what? They can't, so they lie and say, "Those are my parents, we just don't look alike. I take after my grandparents."

We spend most of our life living a lie and trying to forget the past and live for the future and more to come, hoping that no one will ever find out the truth and the skeletons that we've hidden in our closet for so long that we start to think it's the truth.

As I matured and was able to understand and identify with my feelings, I then knew it was nothing that I did or nothing I could've done to prevent this from happening, but it would be my fault if I was to let being a foster child hinder my growth in the world and becoming a successful person.

> *"It wasn't easy living in a new home with different people who have different ways. You don't know how they're going to treat you, but you hope they'll treat you as if you're their own."*
>
> — *Aysheia Monique Carson*

As I've grown up in age and mind, I now have a new addition to my life, a little baby boy whom I must live for and make a future for, explaining to him that no matter what trials and tribulations the world has to offer, the Lord will make a way.

Yvette Martin

My name is Aysheia Monique Carson. I'm 21 years old. I've been living with the Carson family for 15 years. When my brother, Kino, and I first came to the Carsons' home, I was scared and very protective of my little brother (he was only eighteen months, and I was 6). I can't say much about how I felt about Mr. and Mrs. Carson, but I can say they treated us very kind as they welcomed us into their home. It wasn't easy living in a new home with different people who have different ways. You don't know how they're going to treat you, but you hope they'll treat you as if you're their own.

There's all kinds of questions that run through your mind when you're a foster child like my brother, Kino, and I once were. On the other hand, being adopted makes a big difference. It gives you a feeling of really belonging to the people you've been placed with, of being wanted and loved by people who saw you in need and opened their hearts and their home for you to go on and live a halfway normal life.

Speaking of normal, I'm not that normal, because I have epilepsy and other major problems, and I didn't know that until I had a seizure one day at school. I hate having this illness because it sure can make you different and tend to feel sorry for yourself, not wanting to do anything with your life because you are put down and laughed at. Many people don't understand seizures or know what to do when a seizure occurs.

Being adopted is really nice now, yet there is much I am still learning to live with.

Aysheia Monique Carson

How I Feel About Being an Adopted Child

Now let me tell you how I feel,
About this adoption deal.
I feels nothing and I total disagree, on
writing a book and having a movie about me or
this family.
Now my Mom said to tell the truth,
So I'm not gonna lie cause it wouldn't
be cool.

I was only eighteen months so you see
Don't expect to get a lot out of me.
But now there's one thing that I'd like
to say,
That no one knows and I'd like to
keep it that way.
Now don't get me wrong, I thank God
that she picked me out of her own occupation,
But then I don't think that the whole world
should know our situation.

Don't take a picture of me cause I ain't
with it,
and all I want to do is just forget it.
Now I don't know about
anyone else's deal
But I just told you how I feel.

Kino Carson

Sam and Margaret Francis married in 1986. This is Sam's fifth marriage and Margaret's first. They have a son Augustus. Sam has three grown children from previous marriages. Both Sam and Margaret are artists.

What's it like to be married to Sam Francis? What's it like to be married to an older man?

The impossible questions.

What is it like to be married to the artist? What is it like to be married to the man?

It is like trying to describe one's world in a grain of sand.

To be married to the artist is as wonderful as one would expect. Artists are forever young. They recreate themselves because they are involved in the creative process itself. Sam is multifaceted, so life is really full and interesting. Yes, I am married to my guru, but I do mother him just the same.

To be married to the man on a day-to-day basis is probably the same as in any other marriage. The age disparity means the giving of my physical energy to him, but he gives back spiritual energy to me. He encourages me, he is my rock, he is my island.

He says that he is a bad parent. Well, he may have been, but now I would say that he's much more than just a parent to his children. I see it in their eyes, not only the fear and trepidation that a strong father can generate, but also I see them listening to him because he is a leader, someone to hang onto for every word because peppered among everyday conversation, he does bestow upon all of those around him words of infinite and eternal wisdom to be gathered up in the palm of your hand.

Margaret Francis

Love is the Source of Life. Love is at the Hidden Heart of All Miracles. Look into your Heart and Watch the Sun Rise.

I feel great about having a child at this time in my life. It's different from when I had children when I was younger. I don't know how—a new life is just as deep a mystery, but there's nothing troublesome about it. I'm just as bad a parent as I always was. I see Augustus' coming into the world as a cosmic event. It's only since Carl Jung's incursion into the unconscious that these kinds of things were really opened up. If you study all of the psychologies and philosophies of the world, it's always been that way. It's so hard to talk about these things and make any rational sense out of them. Actually, I don't want to be rational. We're talking about something very irrational, a mystery.

For me a woman has always been ageless. I don't feel any different about this marriage than any other marriage. It's like marrying your mother, or better said, putting yourself in the position of being the servant of the Lord, the Lord meaning the face of God is a woman. You never get away from that relationship. The mother is always with you until the moment you die, whoever you are. Every woman has that eternal quality. Margaret is special in this sense to me. Men always think of women as being complete.

I see God as the Mother of Creation.

Sam Francis

Sam, 64, and Margaret Francis, 36, and their son, Augustus, seven months old. (1987)

Robin Jurs and Barbara Allen are a lesbian couple who celebrated their long-term commitment to one another at a ceremony in 1985 amidst more than 100 family and friends. In this commitment ceremony they shared their thoughts, feelings, and lifelong promises with one another. The ceremony was a public statement to their friends and family and the world that lesbians can and do claim a place in the tradition of marriage. They now have two children, Hannah and Cody; Barbara gave birth to one of the children and Robin to the other. Their sperm donors are acquaintances of theirs and do not participate in parenting their children. Barbara and Robin co-parent both children emotionally and now legally due to a formal adoption process. They consider themselves the "all-American, nontraditional family." Robin owns and directs a childcare center and Barbara is a chiropractor in private practice.

My family...our family...and then some extended family. What is pictured here is only a small part of family to me. I grew up the fifth in the line of six children in a family that manifested many of the traditional burdens and rewards of American family life. We have fortunately remained close over the years with our occasional ups and downs and family feuds.

Today, I can say that my deep commitment to family has grown out of my experience from childhood—of being trusted, valued, and cared for as a member of my family and as a person. Today, I also wear some of the scars I inherited from working hard to live according to my parents' expectations of me. In sorting through what belongs to them and what is my own, I have gained insight and appreciation for a family that worked hard to make sense out of a world that wants us all to believe that "Father knows best."

Being a parent myself has always been a given for me. I am lesbian. As my identity as a lesbian emerged in my 20s, I feared for the future of that vision of a family to call my own. I felt ricocheted between my own commitment to having a family, however that may happen, and the world's opinion that family happens when one is married in the conventional manner. As I came out of the closet as a lesbian more fully, I felt the promise of creating a family grow strong within me and more real each day. I believed that I would find a way to form a loving partnership with a woman and keep family, including children, alive in my life. And alive it is!

In my dating days, a friend admonished me not to proclaim on a first date, "Hi, my name is Robin, and I want to have children." I heeded her advice and waited until the second date! On the second date with Barbara it was cinched, we both wanted children. So here we are today, two children and two moms! I call us the "all-American, nonTraditional family." Not always an easy combo, but a richly rewarding one. We have one girl, Hannah, one boy, Cody, two parents (one Mommy, one Mama), a dog, six fish, and a bird. We even have a station wagon!

Friends have always been easily and naturally incorporated into my family, as a child, and now, enlarging the circle and enriching lives. Thus, my commitment to community as an extension of family. Our immediate family is part of a larger community of friends, women and men, gay and straight, with and without children. We laugh, cry, eat, play, and share the ups and downs of life together. Truly, we would be at a great disadvantage without each other. We have grown to depend upon the network of love and support our families have created. It helps expand our world view. It gives

HANNAH

Robin

Barbara

Cody

Robin Jurs, 42, and Barbara Allen, 39, and their daughter, Hannah Jurs-Allen, 4, and son, Cody Jurs-Allen, fourteen months old. (1991)

> *"My heart says, 'We are falling in love.'"*
>
> — *Hannah Jurs-Allen*

us perspective when blinded by the limits we set for ourselves, and security when "all-American" and "non-traditional" do not mix.

As a family, we recently *celebrated* the completion of a bulky adoption process that resulted in making Barbara and me *both* the legal parents of *both* of our children. I gave birth to one and Barbara gave birth to the other. The adoption made legal what has been our intent and practice from the start. Our children have two loving and legal parents.

Among our greatest challenges are those that lie ahead as our children grow up and go out into a world that does not often affirm our lesbian lifestyle...a choice that we as their moms have made but that affects them deeply. As parents, we strive *not* to determine the outcome of our children's lives. However, we cannot help but wonder, what will our children's friends think about our family? What will our children face as others view our family as different? How will our children respond? Will our children find the love and acceptance we all seek from outside the boundaries of our own family as well as from within? Our hope is that our family is helping to create a world where that question brings a resounding "YES" and where differences are viewed as enriching—a world where "Father does not have to know best" because we all trust, respect, and care for one another.

Robin Jurs

I am a passionate lover of nature. On one backpacking trip with a special friend, I was standing with arms outstretched, giving thanks for the remarkable view. Standing there on a 10,000-foot mountain, breathing the clear air, inhaling the beauty of the blue sky, the deep and varied greens of the trees, and the clearness of the Sierra lake. A natural, grand view that filled my heart and soul. I turned to see where my friend was and, to my surprise, he was doing the same thing—standing with arms outstretched, giving thanks and filling himself with the beauty and gifts of nature.

I am a passionate mother. Just as I have filled my being with the natural beauties of this earth, so too, my family has filled me with love and joy. A favorite time for me is tucking Hannah into bed, hearing her reflections of the day, and giving and getting extra snuggles and hugs and kisses. And with Cody, holding and rocking his soft, two-year-old body, feeling the wiggles melt into slumber. There are, of course, difficult times too, but they are far outweighed by the gift and magic of childhood and parenting—my children fill me just as the spirit of the mountains does.

I am a passionate lover of music. When I was in high school I was very involved in drama and music. There was a song from *South Pacific* that I remember well, for it touched my heart as much then as it does now. The lyrics: "You've got to be taught to hate and fear/ You've got to be taught from year to year/ It's got to be drummed in your dear little ear/ You've got to be carefully taught." Those words have stayed with me over the years as I have become what is natural for me, a lesbian and a mother. Being a lesbian is my true nature, just as there is the truth of nature that provides us with melting snow forming cascading waterfalls.

Robin and I had a commitment ceremony is 1985 where we shared out promises with each other. One of my promises to her was, "I will always hold you dear to my heart when the world batters us with judgment." It is a promise I gave to her then, and that I extend to my children now. I promise to always teach my children that different is not bad; that the beauty of nature and that which is natural to the self is the honest way of life. Loving and being loved is really quite simple.

Barbara Allen

Hannah, what does your heart tell you about our family?

My heart says, "We are all falling in love."

Hannah Jurs-Allen

Karen McKie and Barry Krisberg married in 1971. As a biracial couple with different religious and cultural backgrounds, they pay careful attention to encouraging their sons, Moshe and Zaid, to take pride in their multicultural and racial diversity. Karen and Barry are also acutely aware of the racism their children may face. Karen is a homemaker and artist, and Barry is a criminologist.

In Berkeley there are so many biracial families and children therein that the glare of unconventionality is diminished. However, I do think about my choice to marry outside my race, and to have children as a part of that marriage, more now than ever. As my children get older and bump up against the outside world, I am concerned that they be able to define themselves according to the strength and abiding love of our family, and the historical strength and endurance of their races and cultures, rather than allowing themselves to be defined by the limits of others. I worry that others will try to make them choose to identify with one part of their heritage over the other.

We try to infuse our boys with a sense of pride in their racial and cultural heritages. Moshe and Zaid are from two groups of people who have consistently and invaluably contributed to humanity. My concern is that they know their history, their worth, and that they claim it and accept responsibility for it.

As for the way the marriage affects me—sometimes I wonder if Barry's unorthodox (but, exceedingly wise) choice might be viewed negatively by others in terms of his career, and that is painful. This thought comes rarely and usually when there's a halo of perversity around my head. It's hard to say or give examples of occasions when it's come up with others because it doesn't "come up," it's much more subtle than that. At business or social functions people don't say, "Okay, Barry and Karen, how the hell did you two decide to lose your minds and try this charade?" But what does happen is that we are asked quite often, "How did you two meet?" And no matter how lively the conversation around us, the attending silence is almost brittle with expectancy.

From experiences like this and the well-masked (usually) but clear surprise on the faces of people meeting me for the first time (who've not been schooled), it's clear that seeing Barry and me as a couple puts a bump in their comfort zone. Interracial marriages are *still* considered exotic, and the judgment of people who make that choice comes into question. One who leans toward the so called "exotic choice" is in counterpoint to one who proceeds with or values the "tried and true,"—the "adventuresome and frivolous" versus the "upright and solid." So, yes, from time to time I wonder....For myself, I take any implied or

Karen McKie, 41, and Barry Krisberg, 46, and their sons, Moshe, 14, and Zaid McKie-Krisberg, 10 years old. (1991)

> *"As my children get older and bump up against the outside world, I am concerned that they be able to define themselves according to the strength and abiding love of our family, and the historical strength and endurance of their races and cultures..."*
>
> — *Karen McKie*

explicit questioning of my choice as another link in my armor...it feeds my cause... my sense of self. I grew up in a family of women adamant about their spirit force and power...not always to their advantage...but, that's the way of it.

As for working in my home, I come from a family that swallowed the work ethic whole (thousands of years ago) and licked the spoon. Sometimes I find myself in deep conversations with myself about choosing to stay at home with my boys and what this says about being a woman among the women in my family. By the end of these conversations it is clear that it is vitally important to me to raise my own children and that what the women in my family gave, and continue to give me, is the ability to take my vital interests to heart and act on them.

It is important to me to be available to my children and the children of people who don't have the options that I do. Barry is entirely supportive of my vision. I try to be an advocate for my children and others as well. I was brought up to believe that all the children belonged to all the grown-ups. The "me and mine" philosophy is very difficult to abide by. As much as I can, I volunteer in the schools and make sure that our sons know and *internalize* the importance of their education. As an artist and speaker I try to showcase alternative perspectives of the ideals of beauty, strength, courage, and intelligence. As well, I try to be a representative for the children of those people who love them, who help them learn to love themselves, and who look to them for light. I want them to see the light in themselves. I don't know how to teach this to my boys except by example, so I work at home.

Karen McKie

I love being part of a family in which people come from different cultures and backgrounds. We get to share the best of several cultures. I thrive on the closeness and love of family members that pull together during hard times and who are not afraid to expose their most intimate selves to each other. Family life really hits its peak during holidays and special occasions. In our multiracial family the number of these celebrations is much greater. We enjoy Jewish and Christian traditions, and we share with our children those special activities that were part of our unique growing-up experiences. For example, Karen knows most of the details on how to organize a Passover seder dinner. I have come to expect black-eye peas and rice as a "good luck" dinner on New Year's Day.

Because of Karen, I know a lot more about African American history and literature than most of my white colleagues. This multicultural perspective has broadened my education and my flexibility in encountering new situations. I often worry about the racism my children must front, although I am pleased to see how they are creating an identity for themselves. I know that I can never fully comprehend the experience of growing up in a racist society, and so I often follow Karen's lead in terms of how the children must prepare themselves for that battle.

My interracial marriage has not created conflict between Karen and myself. It has been overwhelmingly positive. The only negative that comes up routinely has to do with our family traveling to places that are much less racially tolerant than the San Francisco Bay Area. Back East, we ran into a fair amount of stares and unfriendly attitudes. We certainly consider racial atmosphere when picking vacation spots or when we consider other places where we might live.

Being in a multicultural family has given me a broader perspective about human diversity. I think that I can appreciate a wider range of physical appearances and social styles. For example, I have learned to love spicy foods and enjoy the rich dress colors that favor brown and golden skin tones.

In getting to know Karen's family, I have been exposed to stories and life histories that are very different from my own family background. For example, several of the women in Karen's family did housecleaning work at points in their life. As I grew up, I knew black women who did "day work," but really didn't know (or want to find out) who they were and something about the complexity of their lives and families. I regret being so oblivious to the lives of people around me. I think my marriage has increased my sensitivity to other people.

Another positive aspect of my interracial relationship has been a deepening appreciation of my own rich ethnic heritage. When I was growing up many of my friends (including me) wanted to become WASPs. I went to an Ivy League college and tried to ape the WASP style of dress, speech, and artistic sensibilities as closely as I could. My multicultural family life has caused me to seek the value in my own cultural heritage, to read and learn more, and to be proud of my uniqueness. In my view, a multicultural family can only work if both parents give their children a strong sense of two strong cultural traditions that they represent. In this way the children can choose what appeals to them and mix and match concepts and traditions that will provide them strength.

Barry Krisberg

From the start, I mean back in preschool, I, Moshe McKie-Krisberg, thought that I was Black, and nothing else but Black. I mean, I looked Black, my hair was kinky, my skin was colored, and besides, all the other kids who had anywhere near the same skin color as me were Afro-American. Another thing that bugged me about me was that I thought I had about the funniest name in the world. I got nicknames like: Mush, Mish-Mosh, Moshe potatoes, and Mushy Banana.

Well, enough about me, let's talk about being part of a family that is a racial mix. I don't think being part of this family is any different than any other family. Except the rules are much stricter and they aren't going to get any looser.

Moshe McKie-Krisberg

I think of my family in a good way. Even though our family is mixed black/white, we still celebrate holidays such as Hanukkah, Christmas, and Passover. Being African-American and white doesn't have good or bad parts because it is like any person.

Zaid McKie-Krisberg

85

Glenda Carter lives with her daughter, Chay'la Carter, in a homeless shelter. Glenda was in a relationship with an Army man when she conceived Chay'la. He married another woman when Glenda was several months pregnant. Chay'la's father is African-American. Glenda suffered physical and emotional abuse while growing up, as well as being sexually molested for years by older brothers, events that haunt her today as an adult. The following statement was taken from a recorded conversation at the time the photograph was being made.

I found myself, at 24, pregnant with Chay'la. When I was younger I was told I couldn't get pregnant, so I never used birth control. Now, Chay'la is the only child that I have, the only child that I will ever have. Being a single parent and being responsible for Chay'la, I decided to have a tubal [ligation] done.

I lived with my mother until Chay'la was eight months old, trying to make ends meet, but to no avail. I couldn't provide for a babysitter and work too. Social welfare paid for my babysitter for the first two weeks and told me to bring in my paycheck stubs. Then the social worker said I made too much money, so they wouldn't pay for my babysitter while I worked. When I was living with my mother, there was no way that I could pay the bills and keep us going.

Chay'la's father was not interested in her at all until recently. He's never seen her, except for a few pictures I sent him last week. The other day he called, and the only reason he called is because when I was six-and-one-half months pregnant he told me he did not love me, and he said he was not her father. I had to have a paternity test done, and now he knows that Chay'la is his child. He still wants to deny it because he married his wife when I was six-and-a-half months pregnant and I feel that he doesn't want his wife to know. He's going to have to pay child support because that's his responsibility. But he also said that he was going to take her from me and that I wasn't providing adequate housing because I was in a shelter for the homeless. I'm afraid of Chay'la's father legally petitioning the courts to take her from me. He has to prove me an unfit mother, but there's no way he can prove me an unfit mother.

I want to get an education. For the first time I can set goals in my life and they are attainable. The reason why is because I have somebody to be responsible for. I investigated all the schools and the different options that I would have available, and this shelter seemed like an excellent way to get started. I want to start a radiologist program. It's a two-year program that offers many opportunities for me. Wherever I go, I could always have a job. Being a radiologist is a well-paid profession, not overly well-paid, but it seems to me that would be better for me and Chay'la than welfare.

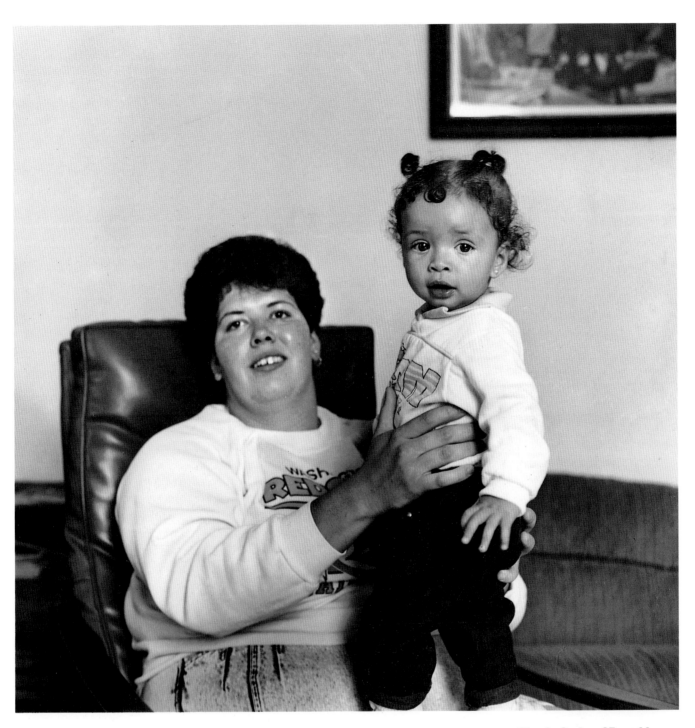

Glenda Carter, 25, and her daughter, Chay'la Carter, nine months old. (1990)

"Once I become financially stable to the point where I can provide a decent home for myself and Chay'la, I would like to volunteer a lot of my time and maybe even help children that come from abused homes."

— *Glenda Carter*

I only went to the eighth grade, but I did go back and get my G.E.D. [General Education Degree]. I also had some training, but just not enough to get a good paying job. It's hard to make a living and support us when I don't have anything. I have no money in the bank; I have nothing. It's real hard being homeless, but I've been through a lot worse. I've experienced a lot of hard times, but Chay'la makes it worthwhile. We're happy because we're together, and this shelter is awful good. They took us in without a second thought. I can't tell you enough about how much I love this child.

When I was a child, I was molested by my older brothers. I was very young, about 5. It was a very long and hard road. My oldest brother is ten years older than me, and the brother after him is about seven years older than me. They were quite a bit older, and out of fear, I didn't say anything. I also felt a lot of guilt, like I had done something wrong. My oldest brother also beat me terribly. My mother thought there was something wrong, something was going on, and she talked to my father about it, and she got beat by my father. He was drunk and abusive anyway.

My parents divorced when I was about 9. Then my mother and my younger brother and I moved to West Virginia. Mom struggled very hard to try and make ends meet, to work every day and provide for me and my younger brother. She couldn't provide because she wasn't making enough money to adequately supervise the well-being of me and my younger brother. Therefore, we were in and out of children's homes.

I had become very promiscuous, and I made a reputation for myself in a very little town. I thought I couldn't get pregnant because I did wrong or because there may have been damage. I was so young [when molested]. When I got to be about 18, I realized that I had to do something to save my sanity. I told my best girlfriend; I let her be my ears. I told her everything [about being abused]. I just told her how much I felt guilty and that I needed to make a different life. I felt robbed and I felt my brothers stole my life. They made a drastic impact on my life, and they had no right to do that. They altered my complete life. I could have had so much better. I still could have things, but it's still not like growing up and getting married and being able to offer something to your husband. I hope to find somebody that's going to be interested in me enough that one day I can have a very healthy and happy relationship.

My brothers have had their histories in and out of prisons, and the younger of the two has a wife and two kids. I don't care to be around him. It's just not a good situation. I went to see my brother, and it just came out that he abused me. He wanted it a secret. He didn't want nobody to know. Maybe in time I will go and have some counseling about this guilt of it all, because it just seems like an overriding feeling sometimes. It's hard, that guilt; it just will not go away, no matter what. You can't imagine how it feels to be robbed. Robbed of a life, a childhood, a dream. Over and over. All the time. A lot of times my mom and dad both worked and we were left alone. I wasn't able to talk about it, but it took years and years of practicing. I have to practice being able to talk about it. Talking to everybody I can about it, I become more comfortable with it. I want to keep it a secret; I want to keep it private because I'm afraid that people are going to look at me differently, act differently towards me, and I'm afraid.

Once I become financially stable to the point where I can provide a decent home for myself and Chay'la, I would like to volunteer a lot of my time and maybe even help children that come from abused homes. Children that have been sexually and physically abused. It just never goes away; you never feel quite whole. The whole point, even about being homeless and about having this baby and trying to do everything—I have just been through so much worse. This is poor, this is difficult, but I get rewards out of this. Just to see Chay'la smile, this gives me something to love. Chay'la is all that I think about—getting my education and providing for her. She gives me something to be responsible for, someone to love. For the first time, I have a reason to live.

Glenda Carter

The Village Oz was a small commune established in 1971 by Lawrence (Redwood) and Margot (Savitri) Kroll. The Kroll's left their home and jobs in the city seeking a new life for themselves and their three children. Six other families joined the Kroll's on their commune in Northern California. The Kroll family dissolved the commune in 1984 and moved back to San Francisco. Lawrence is now a professor of computer science and Margot teaches t'ai chi. Their son, Jon Kroll, is a television producer. Zoey Kroll is a student at Yale University and Panda Kroll is a desktop publishing expert. Panda's husband, Kevin Volkan, is a psychologist.

I remember with great pleasure our outdoor shower of rainbowed drops overlooking the same river I knelt by to draw water, afterwards seeking a t'ai chi path up the slippery alder-root tangled bank. Being an earth mother in the early years meant a typical ten-minute walk to meals turned into hours long with a one-and-a-half year old who stopped to examine dandelions, deer trails, sheep droppings, jays and thimble berries. My daughter, Zoey, taught me to observe nature closely, meditatively. She taught me to climb trees! The other adults had teenagers like my eldest two and, to my disappointment and chagrin, they rarely helped me care for Zoey. I did love our closeness.

My husband enhanced the earthly living by inviting hundreds of inspiring teachers from diverse philosophies, arts, and mental and physical therapies to visit and teach at the commune. He surveyed while I was able to become a disciple for the duration of each workshop. Throughout my explorations, my family, nature, and t'ai chi were constants. At first any loneliness from rural isolation was offset by the loving, stimulating support of my dynamic communal friends. We were all in a 24-hour-a-day college of awakening mystical seeking while enacting (with a high degree of creative nurturing) normal responsible roles as parents, spouses, and homebuilders.

Within our family and the commune, our children were treated with loving respect in their own searches for inspiration and involvement. There was great benefit for the kids having role models other than parents to turn to when blood family communications were at low ebb. The drawbacks to living with explorers on the cusp of cultural change were the many confusions over when it was liberating to let go of old standards of behavior and when it was wise to adhere to them. I couldn't trust my parents' views and my new peers were as diversely confused as well. When we moved back to the city, we were all more comfortable with tighter limits we set for Zoey. Luckily, my two eldest emerged strong and wonderful despite many misjudgments on our part! The rigors of our chosen mode of life—fording the often swollen river, keeping balanced while repairing steeply pitched roofs, walking home through the woods in the dark, alone, combined with the intellectually stimulating commune environment—equipped our kids to be exceptionally realized people. Creative, kind and effective, as teenagers they were able to function in Africa, Paris, and Rome as easily as back home.

Eventually the alternate lonely winters and over-ampted summers of being hosts to kids at drama camp, witches, zen monks, massage therapists, musicians and African dancers grew tiresome, and we moved to San Francisco. Though I miss my heart's home 'mid pristine nature, I have found many almost private beautiful parks here in the city. I enjoy the concentration on my art (t'ai chi) that is only possible in a large metropolis where can be found the leading masters in this esoteric field, as well as many peers also involved in advanced study. I am glad to be out from under the sometimes invasive influence of the commune and to be independently teaching, as opposed to second in command at the land. I feel I am fulfilling a spiritual duty to repay the universe for having the chance to live for 13 years in the magical, mystical, nurturing setting of Oz.

At this point I see my role as parent to be a loving friend and blood-related explorer from the older generation who has likely "been there" and can listen supportively, often without anything very helpful to say. I am in awe of the way my kids are manifesting and look forward to the continuing inspiration of their development.

Margot Savitri Kroll

I moved to the woods of Northern California with my family when my children were young. Working as a teacher at a university seemed boring at the time. I was too young to settle down in a permanent position; there were worlds to explore. Friends talked about the back-to-the-land movement as a great adventure. My wife and I purchased a country property on a river and forested property many miles from any big city. When I sent out a newsletter inviting people I knew to come share with us, I was amazed at the response. About six families formed a commune on our land and built individual homes not within hearing distance or in sight of each other. In the central barn we set up a community kitchen and at the time it was a good balance of privacy and cooperative living. We sent our children to the local three-room schoolhouse and began planting our big garden.

After a few years of this, we grew impatient with the community needs. We just wanted to live our life and be left alone for a while. Most of the original people had separated and moved on. After all, they did not own the land. There had been a constant change of people living with us and, even with the frequent meetings, the intensity of involvement was no longer at a peak. Savitri and I were extremely family-centered and grew closer as we struggled to find a place for ourselves in the small town country setting. While we had savings, it was always hard to find meaningful work and income. We tried workshops, camps for adults and children, teaching, and small business. Our two older children left to go to college. After 13 years of living without electricity or telephone at home, we saw that we were starting to get stuck. I accepted a position teaching again and we moved with our youngest child back to San Francisco.

Life seems a lot simpler since our return to civilization. I don't spend time making fires to warm up my house or fuss with lanterns for the night. The economic situation seems much clearer. I am not so critical of my job. In fact, I am glad to have one that I enjoy. I go to work every day, put my energy into the job I am paid for, and at the end of the month I get a nice paycheck. The city is expensive, but the exchange seems very clear. Our youngest child has gone off to college, and Savitri and I are the close couple we were when we first met. It's romantic. Our children come home on vacations and weekends, and we are happy to have the family together again.

I have become fascinated with new topics in computer graphics and technology, and these interests are totally involving. I think I was lacking intellectual stimulation in the country. The Saturday night movie and Bookmobile were hardly enough to challenge my mind. A bonus to my work is that the university provides the tools I need for this research.

In retrospect, I think that the lifestyle we experienced was background for the solid family we have always been. My university colleagues tell me that I am quite the eccentric being, having lived in the woods for so long. They don't really know what I did. What they see is a hard-working professional with a creative streak. In spite of my alternative credentials, I have always seen myself as an adventurer, a father, a provider, and a husband. Scratch a "hippy" and you may find a fun-loving solid citizen!

Lawrence Redwood Kroll

When we first decided to move to Oz, I was eight years old and very unhappy about the decision. I was forced to give up all of my material possessions (and I had a lot of them) and move into a 100-year-old barn without a roof. This was not my idea of a good time.

The first couple of months were quite difficult for me, but soon the experience of living without electricity and running water became a way of life, and since there were other kids living there, we had a sort of "New York Attitude"—we were all in this together.

The Village Oz Commune in 1978. Margot (Savitri) Kroll, 42, sits in the front of the hot tub with son, Jon Kroll, 16, to her right. Margot's husband, Lawrence (Redwood) Kroll, 43, stands at the right in the rear of the hot tub. Others in the photo were members of the commune.

The Kroll family in 1990. Margot (top) and Lawrence Kroll, and their children (from top); Panda Kroll, 30, and her husband, Kevin Volkan, 31, Zoey Kroll, 20, and Jon Kroll, 28.

> *"My years in the city have been satisfying socially, scholastically, and artistically. I attribute this to my life in the country where change and challenge were a daily experience."*
>
> — *Zoey Kroll*

After our attempt to start our own school, we joined the local school, which created an entirely new set of challenges. Not only were we trying to adjust to this entirely new way of life, but at the same time we were trying to remain integrated with the world outside via the local school. The locals saw us as an invasion and seemed to feel threatened, and this continued for about five years until I entered high school. During that time, more than 100 people lived at Oz, and we went through every diet, health fad, seminar, guru, and drug imaginable. Oz residents were affected by EST, Esalen, Arica, Baba Ram Das, and the Dalai Lama.

Our family remained a constant throughout these changes. Every Wednesday night was family night, also known as "Family Fight Night," as the week's tensions all seemed to be released in this one three-hour period. The fight would find its way into the evening like clockwork about an hour after dinner. Favorite topics were who would do the dishes, poor bridge play, chores, the dirty house, and misuse of Dad's things (comic books, Star Trek phaser guns, etcetera).

At the time I entered high school, we started running a summer camp (as a family), and this put us in the interesting position of having to "set an example for others". We knew nothing of manners (etiquette) or "proper behavior." While this would shock some people, most welcomed it as a breath of fresh air. The camp environment allowed me to blossom as a teacher and a leader. As the focus of the summer camps began to shift to drama, which was my department, I began to assume more of a leadership role in the camp as a whole. My father and I squared off frequently over issues involving the camp. He seems to write these off as "typical director/producer struggles," but as I am now functioning as both a director and a producer, I can say with some authority that we were both functioning inappropriately in those roles. Good producers and directors know how to get what they want through tact and diplomacy; we showed neither. Again, these experiences were tremendously helpful in developing my working skills. All of these early life experiences have led me to be an extremely gregarious person.

Jon Kroll

After living in a commune for my first 13 years and canoeing to school every day, I feel prepared for anything. Communal life taught me at an early age to love people from all different backgrounds and to work through my differences with them. I took an active part in the self-contained community. When I could barely reach the table, I kneaded bread for the group supper and collected miner's lettuce in the forest for the salad.

This sharply contrasted with the experiences of the kids I went to school with, who were raised on Wonder Bread and American conservatism. At times, I resented my home and family. I thought living without a television (we had no electricity) and a telephone might stunt my growth. As a vegetarian in a school full of cowboy-booted, tobacco-chewing farm kids, my values were constantly challenged. I cringed when my mother, wearing a patchwork dress over tie-dyed, flared pants, picked me up from school. When would my parents realize the sixties were over? Finding a balance between two conflicting environments encouraged me to think for myself, not just listen to my friends at school or my family at home.

Although I sometimes wished I had a "normal" family, living among eccentric idealists exposed me to a snowstorm of new theories. Acupuncture, tarot cards, encounter groups, yoga, Tibetan Buddhism, dream workshops, and self-sufficiency were not just concepts spoon-fed to me by the media; I experienced them. This stimulating commune set in an isolated town gave me irrevocable strength, curiosity, and powers of adaptability.

Eventually the same isolation that had fostered the development of inner strengths began to limit me. After ten years of going to school with people who thought a trip to the drive-in was a cultural experience, I wanted more intellectual stimulation from school. By logical arguments, screams, and notes under pillows, I persuaded my parents to move to San Francisco in the middle of my freshman year.

I switched from a school of 200 Caucasians to a school of 2000 kids, divided equally between Caucasians, Blacks, Hispanics, and Asians. Again, I learned to cross accepted cliquish boundaries by mingling with students of all races and interests. I took advantage of the resources in the city by taking classes at museums and theater schools, performing at a comedy club, volunteering at a brain research laboratory, and using the extensive libraries for research.

My years in the city have been satisfying socially, scholastically, and artistically. I attribute this to my life in the country where change and challenge were a daily experience.

Zoey Kroll

Ben Xu and Xiaowei Shi were born in China and met when they were studying at the University in Suzhou. In 1985 Ben came to the United States to study for a doctorate in English literature. Six months later his wife, Xiaowei, arrived in the U.S. to work on her doctorate in education. Their 3-year-old son, Yixing, remained in China, living alternately with his two sets of grandparents while his parents settled in the U.S. Yixing had not seen his parents for two years when they were reunited in 1988 in Massachussets. Ben is an English professor who specializes in contemporary literary criticism and ethnic literature, and Xiaowei teaches English as a second language while completing her university studies.

Born in China, educated both in China and in America and now being a professor in America, I find myself constantly puzzled by the question, "Who am I?" My past experience in China can define me only in rather superficial terms, partly because that part of my life experience now exists only in my memory, and partly because there was really nothing personally unique about that experience. Like almost everyone else of my generation, I was sent to the country to be re-educated before I had finished high school. I worked as a farmer for almost eight years and became a university student only after the Cultural Revolution was over. It was when I was a graduate student in Suzhou University that I met Xiaowei, who was also studying in that University and later became my wife.

Before I came to the United States in 1985, I was the only doctoral student in the English Department of Fudan University and was working on my dissertation. Fudan is a great research university, and I would like to go back and teach there. But we've got a son of 9. Yixing, our son, is too Americanized to feel comfortable going back to China. If it is not easy for me to answer the question, "Who am I?" how much more difficult it would be for Yixing to answer the same question! He knew about 2,000 Chinese characters when he came to the States four years ago, but now he can barely speak Chinese. The Chinese schools are very competitive. Since Yixing has lost much of his Chinese, he could have a hard time trying to get into a good high school if he went back to China.

We moved from Amherst, Massachusetts to California in August 1991. This is not an easy move for us. Amherst is almost like our hometown. I miss my good friends there. If I was uprooted six years ago when I came to this country, moving to California represents a second time of being uprooted. Moving from one place to another, I feel constantly uprooted and transplanted in new soil. The experience is not bad in itself, but it gives me the feeling of having no anchor to tie my identity

Ben Xu

I entered high school during the Cultural Revolution, just in time to be a Red Guard and then to be sent to the countryside to be re-educated by the poor and lower-middle peasants. This was when I began to taste the uncertainty of life in China.

I had a happy childhood. As a kid in primary school, I was too young to understand and share my parents' worries caused by the constantly changing political situation in China. I became a Red Guard when the Cultural Revolution broke out, but before long I was

Ben Xu, 41, Xiaowei Shi, 40, and their son, Yixing Xu, 9 years old. (1991)

> *"I feel constantly uprooted and transplanted in new soil....it gives me the feeling of having no anchor to tie my identity."*
>
> — *Ben Xu*

kicked out because my father was accused of "taking the capitalist road." He was imprisoned for more than four years. I was sent to a remote village to be re-educated and that re-education cost ten years of my life. Experiencing the hard life of Chinese peasants, I did learn a lot from those simple and uneducated people. With the end of the Cultural Revolution, I became one of the lucky people to enter colleges that had practically been shut down for ten years.

The college life was not as exciting as I expected, but it is unforgettable. It was then that I realized my dream of college education, which I had since I was a high school student, and it was then that I fell in love with Ben. The first day I was in the college, I was assigned to share a desk with Ben in our classroom. We sat together three classes a day and six days a week. I don't remember exactly when we started to love each other, but I suspect it was pretty soon. I got special permission to marry Ben and had our son Yixing a few months after graduation.

Ben came to study in the United States in 1985, and I came to join him six months later. Yixing stayed back in China with his grandparents. I soon became a graduate student myself. Again Ben and I studied in the same university. In order to survive in this new land, I first did housekeeping and cleaning for a few families and then worked in a restaurant. Then I worked in primary and high schools, first as a tutor, then as a teacher's aide, and finally as a high school teacher. Yixing came to join us two years after I came to this country. He got adjusted to the new environment much faster than Ben and me. Last summer we moved to the West Coast because of Ben's new job. I am writing my doctoral dissertation this year, and I hope I can start teaching again as soon as I finish my studies.

I have had all ups since my arrival in this county and have not had any downs yet. I feel this is the land for me to realize my dream, my American dream. I hope Yixing will get his education in this country. It is for Yixing's future, if not for anything else, that I want to stay here permanently.

Xiaowei Shi

My name is Yixing, and I am 9 years old. I was born in Shanghai, China, in the year 1982. When I was 5 years old I came to the United States to live with my mother and father. My parents love me very much, and I love them, too. My grandparents came from China to visit me. It is very nice to have them here. My parents cannot play with me since they are always busy. Now I have my grandparents to play with.

I started playing violin when I was 6 and practiced one hour each day. Now, since I am older, I play violin for two hours instead of just one. I practice violin twice a week at school and go to my violin teacher on Saturday. I enjoy music a lot. My favorite subjects in school are math, science, and P.E. My favorite kind of game is kickball because I get to kick and run and have lots of fun. I learn to read and write Chinese at home, and I also take Spanish classes after school. I like reading chapter books in my spare time. I like playing Nintendo when I finish work. I moved here to California about four months ago.

I like California better than Massachusetts since the weather is great and I have many new friends. I had my best Halloween this year going trick-or-treating with my new friends. I got a lot of candy and some little Halloween toys. I love Halloween, but I like Christmas better. I get lots of presents each Christmas.

I want to stay here in America because I have a lot more friends here than I did in China. My four best friends are Liam, Noah, Chris, and Hugo. Liam is the first friend I ever made here in the U.S.A. He was in my first grade class. After I came here to California he came to visit me and we went to Yosemite National Park. Hugo is from China just like me. He and I visited each other a lot when I was in Massachussets, since his father is my father's best friend. Noah is the first friend I made here in California. Chris is my new neighbor here. He is a very nice boy. He plays with me and teaches me Spanish sometimes. I miss my friends in Massachussets, and sometimes I wonder, "Will I ever see them again?"

Yixing Zu

Robert Meyer, a single parent, adopted Juliet at birth through an attorney who specializes in private party adoptions. The birth mother was chronically alcoholic and homeless, and a part of the adoption agreement was that Robert would take care of all of her needs and prenatal care. Robert was present for Juliet's birth. She was born premature and weighed less than four pounds. Robert is the executive director of a fund-raising agency for a treatment facility for chemically dependent children.

Our family came to be as a sort of dream. I was a single man, working in a well-paying position as the executive director of a fund-raising agency for a residential treatment facility for chemically dependent kids. I am a substance abuser, that is, a chemically dependent person recovering from addiction to alcohol and drugs. I had just purchased my home and was wanting to give something back to society. At that time I was considering becoming a foster parent. I approached the social service department of the county where I live and was directed to the "fostadopt" program.

To make a long story short, while I was doing a home study for the program, a friend of mine who noticed what I was doing asked me if I might be interested in a newborn child. She had a friend who was pregnant and wanting to give up her child for adoption, but hadn't chosen a family or parent yet. We met, both had good feelings about the other, and entered a contract. This was all done with an attorney who specialized in adoption through private parties. Also, it should be mentioned that the birth mother was chronically alcoholic, 39 years old, homeless, and without much prenatal care. She continued to drink throughout her pregnancy. A large part of our arrangement was that I took care of all of her needs as well as the unborn baby's. This was a high-risk pregnancy and very stressful.

Juliet was born premature, weighing three pounds, thirteen ounces. I was there for the delivery, which was not normal, as planned. Juliet was in the intensive care nursery for five days, and came home with me after she reached four pounds. She was born very small because of the alcoholism and prematurity and she's still not on the charts. At 2 years of age she weighs eighteen pounds, but developmentally she's beyond the charts in her intelligence. She's seen a lot of people who work in the genetic field with high-risk children, but her placement among other "normal" kids is that she is even or advanced.

The difference between the way I was raised and the way I raise Juliet are far apart and the same in many ways. I sleep with Juliet a lot and, for the first six months of life together, we shared the same bed. This was something that never existed in the home I grew up in. Also, Juliet stays up a lot longer than I did as a child because it is our only time together after a long day of work and day care. I was raised at

Robert Meyer, 33, and his daughter, Juliet, twenty-one months. (1989)

"Juliet has taught me so much about life....The largest lesson is how precious this gift is and how important it is to not take life for granted."

— *Robert Meyer*

home by my mother, who took care of me and the household while my father worked all day. Today I have to find the best substitute for the job of child care, and it is away from the house. We wake before the sun, get dressed, and drive twenty miles to the day care. I go to work for nine hours and pick her up and drive home in traffic. We return home after sunset. Lots of our meals are bought at restaurants as a means of saving time.

Juliet is part of me. We go almost everywhere together, not only for her entertainment but to my social events and affairs. I take Juliet along to as many things as possible, much to the displeasure of others who don't want to hear from an infant. I spoil my child with all sorts of extras, and I work an additional part-time job to afford this luxury. I feel as if I spend more time with Juliet than my parents did with me. I'm not sure how accurate this is, since I don't remember much from my twos and threes. But, as a single parent, I am the sole person responsible to feed, change, doctor, pick up, drop off, etcetera.

Juliet and I have created a bonding with each other that is stronger than any I ever had with either of my parents, as well as a friendship. The type of parenting that I practice is that of learning by experiment and experience. I try to be as direct as you can with an infant. I try to listen and answer, not yell and shut down with anger and frustration.

The most difficult part about being a single parent is not enough time, but this is probably the same for families with more than one parent, time to be with my child as well as time to be by myself. I see my role as parent as a great job. I'm both a parent and a friend. We both teach each other about life and how it works. Sometimes I'm more amazed with what Juliet knows than with what I can teach her. Watching the process of growing and learning from the beginning is a wonderful experience that fulfills my life greatly.

Juliet has taught me so much about life that I could write a book, and I just might some day. The largest lesson is how precious this gift is and how important it is to not take life for granted. There is so much to learn, and time quickly passes as a parent. I turn around and find myself angry that I didn't record the event or take a picture of something. Every day new and wonderful things happen. Even the worst illnesses we face have lessons that keep us growing together and make us stronger.

It has not been more difficult for me to raise a daughter than a son. I believe that it would be just as hard to raise a child of my own sex. People give me strange looks when they hear the whole story, and some people are just close-minded. That is the most difficult—it just hurts to have people who are strangers talk down to me or tell me something that I don't need to hear. Raising a baby girl, I get advice from everyone—from people in the supermarket to the doctor's office. I just have to be polite and take what's good and leave the rest behind. I get a lot more help from the staff of the children's department in the department store than I do from the pediatric nurses who don't take the time to read the cover of Juliet's file and learn her history. I get sick of hearing, "It's nice to see Dad helping out Mom today," by taking the baby to the doctor or shopping. The hardest part about raising a little girl is that my mother now has a "daughter" (grandchild) that she never had and wants to shower her with gifts and help as much as possible. This is truly a blessing instead of a hardship.

Being a parent is hard. There isn't any way around it. But becoming a parent by choice has some advantages: people know how you waited and wanted a child. It always makes me feel a little stronger when I remember that I don't have to do things alone and that my life has a purpose. Together we can achieve things that others couldn't have dreamed of 25 years ago, maybe even 10 years ago.

Today I look at life a lot differently than before parenthood. I have faith in a power much more powerful than both of us. I believe in being open-minded and positive, and I take time for me. Juliet is the number one reason to stay healthy, get to work, pay the mortgage, and buy food. If Juliet is sick, then I stay home. I am the primary care-giver and must always be available to be with her. I do this without hesitation or a second thought. I have become an unselfish person.

My hopes for Juliet are that she have the ability to continue to get the most out of life, that she will grow up with the courage to challenge things in front of her, and that she will always be able to come to me or others for help and support. I hope that Juliet will have a genuine concern for the things around her and that she will take advantage of all things offered to her. I hope that Juliet will become the type of person that will stay open-minded to new ideas and different ways of life without question. These are the values that I would like Juliet to grow up with and, hopefully, be able to pass on to others as she goes through life. If I were to start all over, I wouldn't change a thing, other than maybe do it once more.

Robert Meyer

(Postscript)

We now have a biological baby brother, Jonathan, born March 1991, and an older brother, Billy, a foster son who is 17 years old. Our family has grown. Juliet is 5 years old now. She is still small, under thirty pounds, and about forty inches tall. Juliet is in great health and continues to amaze almost everyone.

Robert Meyer

Yvonne and Otis Tucker have four chil-dren: Otis III, Terry, Tamia, and Telly. (Otis III is in the Army, stationed in Germany, and was not included in the family photograph.) Yvonne and Otis built a home in 1974 in a Virginia suburb where they raised their children. Yvonne is a middle-school teacher and guidance counselor, and Otis recently took early retirement, at age 53, as a high-school teacher and football coach. Otis now coaches part time and works at home.

In the summer of 1959 I enrolled as a freshman at Shaw University in Raleigh, North Carolina, where I met my husband, Otis. We married August 10, 1964. After five years of marriage, Otis and I had our first child, Otis III. Four years later our second son, Terrin Renard, was born. After three years of parenting two sons, we both agreed that two children were adequate. But much to our surprise, I became pregnant with our only daughter, Tamia Lauvonne, who was born in 1976, followed by another son, Telly DeShawn in 1979. After the fourth child, we made sure this was it.

I grew up in a very small town where everybody in town knew my family, which consisted of me, my sister, who is two and a half years older than me, and my father. Both of my parents were college graduates and worked in the educational field. My mother became seriously ill shortly after my birth and was hospitalized for most of my childhood years. Consequently, I grew up in a home where it was necessary to assume a great deal of independence at an early age. My sister assumed the role of a maternal figure; therefore, we were not very close. Frequent bickering and fighting with my sister made it extremely difficult for the three of us to get into a closely knit family unit.

Two days before my twelfth birthday, my mother passed. This traumatic and unfortunate experience caused me to grow up as a very lonely, shy, quiet, and withdrawn individual with very little or no expression of physical affection toward my father, sister, or maternal grandparents who helped to raise us.

Otis's family was different from mine. His parents did not complete high school. His father was the sole breadwinner until Otis became of school age. Then his mother would work occasionally. Even though Otis's family was poor with little or no extra money, there was a lot of love and closeness among the family members. There was always enough food for the six-member family and his father, who worked as a mechanic for a car dealer, was able to buy a car. They enjoyed frequent outings as a family and supported one another in their school activities. Two children in Otis's family went to college on athletic scholarships and work-study programs.

The family in which our children are growing up cannot be compared to my family or Otis's family. The differences are as follows: we live in an integrated neighborhood in a house much larger and more elegant than Otis's family or my family could afford or even be allowed to own; our children have parents with graduate degrees; our children are exposed to a lot of cultural activities and have the opportunity to broaden their awareness of cultural differences, whereas Otis's and my experiences were limited to our immediate surroundings. Enjoying an extended vacation was a luxury afforded to Black affluence. Today it is almost routine within the Black family.

The most difficult part in our family is trying to juggle the responsibilities of job, home, and family and yet maintain support and involvement in our children's activities. We often find ourselves with very little quality family time. It is also difficult for us to convey to our children that they must develop their own unique personalities and not conform to pressures exerted by friends and classmates.

I see myself as a parent, a friend, an advisor, a disciplinarian, and an avid fan and supporter of my children. Frequently my role used to extend to that of father and mother when Otis's job required a lot of time away from home. When I asked him how he saw his role as a parent at that time he said, "My role as a father is not as difficult as it could be because of the amount of time I spend out of the home. I regard myself as the provider and a supporter for my wife, who handles most of the family matters, particularly those involving the children." Recently, because of a change in the state law, Otis, at age 53, was offered a chance to retire early. He accepted, so now he's coaching football part time and no longer teaching. He says "I'm Mr. Mom around here now. I'm painting, cooking, cleaning house, and repairing things that have needed my attention for years. I'm doing things at my own pace, and I'm enjoying it."

If I were to start over again, I would change the following: we would have had our children closer together and would have completed it at a much younger age. We would have spent more time with our children. We would have started them in school a year later so that they would have acquired more emotional maturity and been more successful in school. We would have had them spend as much time with their maternal grandparents as they did with their paternal grandparents. We would have planned more family-oriented activities.

We hope our children will develop into healthy, wholesome, and successful individuals with the capabilities to enjoy the comforts of life

Yvonne Tucker

Yvonne, 48, and Otis Tucker, 53, and their children, Terry, 17, Tamia, 14, and Telly, 11. (1990)

At the time the first photograph was made, Vicki Noble and Karen Vogel were a lesbian couple rearing Vicki's daughters, Robyn and Brook Ziegler, from a previous marriage. In 1989 the family was photographed again. Vicki and Karen were no longer in a lesbian relationship, but still close friends. Vicki had married Jonathan Tenney and they have a son Aaron Eagle. Vicki's daughters now live on their own, but in the same city. Vicki, Karen, Jonathan, and Jonathan's mother, Marga Tenney, bought an old Victorian house together and live as an extended family. In 1991, Jonathan moved out of the household and lives with his two adult daughters. Aaron Eagle lives half time with Jonathan and half time with Vicki.

The most significant change in my family since we were first photographed in 1978 is the shift of gender in my primary relationships! At that time, I was living with my partner, Karen Vogel, and my two young daughters, and I was thinking of myself as a lesbian separatist. For a period of five years, I actually didn't relate to men in any significant ways at all. It was like a healing fast and served me well. Karen and I were very creative together, and I think we set a very positive tone for raising my girl children through their adolescence. Their friends came around to our house for counseling and a feeling of support. Even though they basically found it weird that we were lovers, they liked the general atmosphere we set up for them in the household during those five years.

In 1983 I married Jonathan Tenney, and for several years we lived with our little boy, Aaron Eagle, and Jonathan's mother, Marga Tenney, as well as my old friend and partner, Karen Vogel. On the surface, it might look like a pretty big change, but inside—to the heart—it has happened all in the flow of things.

Our extended family came together organically, through the course of our varied lives. Karen and I split up for a few years, during which time my girls grew up and moved away, and I met and married Jonathan. Jonathan and I moved to Arizona for a couple of years where Aaron was born, and Karen (who was also living near Phoenix) managed, rather magically, to be present at the birth. Marga Tenney lived with us for a little while during our stay in Arizona and then moved to Seattle. Eventually, Karen moved back to the Bay Area, and so did Jonathan, Aaron, and I. During part of that time, my daughter Brooke lived with us, as did Jonathan's eldest daughter Rachael. Finally, in 1989, Marga came to live with our family, and we decided to buy a house together. Karen expressed an interest in joining us, and there we were, one big happy family in a huge old Victorian house in Berkeley.

Eventually Jonathan and I felt the need to live separately, and he moved out and set up his own home, where his two adult daughters have joined him for a while. Aaron Eagle travels well between our two households, supported and loved by many more people than just his two parents. Marga, Karen, and I continue to live as one of his two households. Both Jonathan and I deeply appreciate sharing our life as Aaron Eagle's parents with other people who cherish him. The support is substantial.

In the ancient cultures of the Goddess that are the focus of my research and writing, men and women did not live together in nuclear families, and children were never raised by a single adult. The varied experiences and living arrangements in my life have provided me with opportunities to experiment. And although I tried very hard to humanize the nuclear family structure and make it work, ultimately I don't believe it is the best form. I am committed to the extended household concept, especially to living in a house with other women while raising children. Aaron is delighted with our home where he has an auntie and a grandma under the same roof with his mother.

My role as a parent is extremely significant to me and always has been. I love being a mother, and I feel stronger for the challenges it has always presented me with. Raising my girls was a wonderful, pioneering process in which I sometimes felt we had thrown away the manual that told how to do it, and we were creating together a new path. Recently my eldest daughter, Robyn, called to tell me how grateful she was for the way I had raised her; she thanked me! What mother doesn't dream of that?

Robyn and Brooke both live in Santa Cruz now, just over an hour from us, and we are closely in touch. They are living their own lives, earning their own money, and I'm very pleased and proud of them. My son, Aaron, is the gift of my middle age. A love-child completely, he came in answer to Jonathon's and my request for a child together. Giving birth to Aaron at home with our family present was one of the great moments of my life, and raising a boy child at this late date is a profound blessing for me. He is a *special* child, having Down's syndrome, and he has

functioned in our lives as a sort of spiritual teacher, as well as a delightful, elfin child. He was the glue that held our relationship together for so long, and now he seems to be the center of our two separate households.

I hope for my children to know who they are and act from that knowledge. I want them to be happy and healthy, and I trust that they will be because they have learned, through being trusted and loved, to trust and love themselves.

If I could change anything, I would change the ways my first two babies were "delivered" in hospital settings that denied us the proper beginnings. I would have my profound spiritual-feminist transformation take place at an earlier date, so that we would be on the right track from the very beginning. But even that seems fated, in the sense that I had my children before I knew what the options for women really were, so there was no conflict for me! *Naturally,* I became a mother. For feminist women later in their development, it is more of a conflict, I think. I would also change some of the early difficulties that put pressure on my girls when I was a single mother under a lot of stress. But I suppose even that has its developmental pluses, who knows? I think I probably wouldn't change much at all. I love my life. I feel very blessed and very grateful. I give thanks every day.

Vicki Noble

*Vicki Noble, 30, her daugh-
ters, Robyn Ziegler, 11, (in
her lap), and Brooke Ziegler,
9, and Noble's partner,
Karen Vogel, 28. (1978)*

Vicki Noble (front center),
Karen Vogel (front left),
Noble's husband Jonathan
Tenny, Robyn Ziegler holding
Aaron Eagle Tenny-Noble, 4,
(Vicki and Jonathan's son),
Marga Tenny (Jonathan's
mother), and Brooke Ziegler.
(1989)

"I am committed to the extended household concept, and especially to living in a house with other women while raising children."

— *Vicki Noble*

I remember a conversation with Robyn and Brooke that was a result of work Vicki and I were doing with them. We were trying to get the kids to respect the moms' space. Vicki used the analogy of baby birds being pushed out of the nest so they could learn to fly. Robyn responded with a story where she had seen the babies crash to the ground.

In retrospect, I feel that we built a nest together and are what I call family. We all flew. And we crash and fly again. One of the extraordinary and wonderful gifts in my life is how the nest we built continues to exist, change, and expand.

I was fortunate to be a part of the birth of Aaron Eagle. There were many great moments during his birth. One that stands out for me was when Brooke was helping her mother breathe through the contractions. They were looking into each other's eyes and Vicki said, "We once did this." I felt my tears of love and healing for the mother and daughter in me that could bond because of seeing and feeling it through Vicki and Brooke.

Now Vicki, Marga, and I are buying a house together. Our story is to be continued as we enter this new era in our family. The self I gave birth to in our family is myself as an artist. I did that with the co-creation with Vicki of the Motherpeace Round Tarot Deck and also in my personal art of woodcarving and doll making. The continuation, growth, and additions to our family help me to have strength and openheartedness, which is the source of my creativity. As a lesbian and an artist with a desire for family and community, this is what I've created for myself.

Karen Vogel

What is unique about my family is that we're such an "extended" family—on my mom's side I have Jonathan as a father, Aaron as the new addition, and two stepsisters. On my dad's side, I have a stepmother and two stepbrothers, and of course there is Robyn, my real sister. We are very close as a family, and I feel that Mom and Jonathan are my friends who I can turn to for support when I need them. The best thing about my family is the strong bond of love we have—I can tell Mom anything without fear of being judged harshly. I admire both Vicki and Jonathan; they make excellent role models. Watching Aaron's birth was one of the greatest experiences I've had, and I feel that Mom has now taught me just about everything you can teach a daughter—she took the fear out of parenting by showing me how to do it.

The only thing I would change is our living situation. I would like us all to live in the same town so I could see them more often. And I wish I got along better with my father and his family, which has always been separate and never felt like family to me—not the good, comfortable family that I have with my mother. We have a lot of love to give each other.

Brooke Ziegler

John Elledge went to Honduras as an Episcopal missionary. While there, he met and married Iris, and together they founded a home for abandoned girls. John legally adopted Iris's children, Dilcia and Danilo, and they moved to the United States. At the time the photograph was made, John and Iris planned to adopt Juan Navarrete, a refugee from El Salvador who had been with them for two weeks, but this did not work out. Iris is a nursing assistant in a nursing home and John is the director of a homeless shelter.

I met Iris at my best friend's house in Honduras, where I was an Episcopal missionary. My best friend was dating Iris's best friend, and we had occasion to get to know one another that way. We had become quite good friends over about ten months and fell in love.

I have really enjoyed my family. Being a stepfather to Danilo and Dilcia has certainly been an enriching experience. I've had to grow up just one step ahead of them, though sometimes their maturity and understanding of the world surpasses mine.

What I love about my family is that we all want the world to be a better place. Iris works with older people in a nursing home to make their lives more comfortable; I run a homeless shelter; and the kids both volunteer at the shelter from time to time. Occasionally however, our idealism doesn't work the way we would like. Our experience with Juan Navarrete is a good example. Juan was a Salvadoran refugee we took into our home and treated like a member of the family. Unfortunately, I feel he took advantage of our family and had to leave on unpleasant terms. We are still angry and disappointed about the situation. Although we will always be more guarded as a result of the experience, we will always be committed to others. That's what makes our family great.

John Elledge

I met my husband in my country, Honduras. We got married and we lived for three years in my country. We worked for the Episcopal Church, and we had the opportunity to create a new hope for abandoned girls. We founded a home which we called Our Little Roses, to which we dedicated ourselves for a year. Later we decided to return to the United States.

It wasn't easy to begin again here. I had to work when I didn't speak any English, but I had to do it, and I had to find a way to do it. I went to the Office of Nursing Assistants at the nursing home in our town. I got a job, and I am still doing the same job. I found a way to enjoy my work, and I was happy because I found more "roses." I call them my big roses, and they are like my second family in the U.S. I still think of them as my second family.

My husband worked for a while and then decided to return to his studies. This made us wonder what we would do financially, because he could only work part time. I remember how sweet my husband was when he didn't want me to have to work, and how I surprised him by working sixteen-hour days, but this was the only way he could go to college. I worked like that for a year.

I remember that John worked as a school bus driver. He finished a year at community college, and we had to move to another place so that he could study international business at the university. At this time I could do nothing about my own studies because I was so tired and working on such a strange schedule. Money was also so tight that we could only afford the primary necessities. A year after we moved, I decided to work on my G.E.D. [General Education Degree]. I had to first learn to read and write in English.

Now I am still struggling to get ahead with the language, my studies, my family, and my job. I thank God that He gave us two fine, sweet children who don't give us any problems and whom we can trust. The whole family is still studying for a better future in this new world that has been hard to get used to.

Iris Elledge

John, 28, and Iris Elledge, 33, and their children, Danilo, 17, and Dilcia Elledge, 13. Juan Navarrete, 18 (left), was living with the family at the time. (1990)

Melanie Stone and Paul Korhummel live together with their son, Nikolai "Bunky" Korhummelstone, and Melanie's daughter from a previous marriage, Noele Guthrie. Melanie and Paul knew each other for ten years before deciding to live together in 1987. They have chosen not to marry. Paul is a designer-builder, Melanie is a gift-shop manager, and Noele is a recent college graduate working as a waitress. Three months after the photograph was made, Melanie, Paul, and Bunky were planning to leave for Asia to spend one to two years traveling around the world.

Paul and I came to live together after about ten years of knowing each other and dating off and on for different periods. I was 41 years old and, having wanted a second child for years, felt secure enough to tell Paul I wanted to try to get pregnant. Two months later we decided to try living together. Three months later I was pregnant.

Having children lets me express my love endlessly and gives me a connection to other families and to the future of the world. Marriage doesn't signify security to me, as my parents divorced, and I did too. Not being married reminds me I am continuing to choose to live with Paul and I do because this relationship enhances who I am and gives me the support to explore more of what I can be. My ex-husband and I have a continuing good relationship because I appreciate him as a person and as a wonderful father to our daughter, Noele. His family has not only continued to love me but has also included Paul and treats Bunky as another grandchild.

A supportive, nourishing environment is what I hope to give to my children in order for them to grow, feeling safe to explore themselves inwardly and expansively in the world. Traveling around the world, I believe, will literally help us all do this. It will give us time together to become closer and to see and feel the different ways people live and relate to each other.

Melanie Stone

I have never been married. I come from a very traditional family of eight children (Catholic) with parents who married for life. My mother was a professional housewife and my father, a government employee.

Although I have always enjoyed children, I had never really envisioned my own.. This may have had a lot to do with being one of the older boys in my family and having to care for my younger brothers and sister. I felt I had already had a family.

Even though I loved being part of a "gang," I can remember that by the time anything was split up eight ways, my share was always too small. I therefore envied smaller families, where the kids got more attention. So I'm happy to have just one child, and I'm enjoying our relationship as it unfolds. I feel very honored to have Nikolai as a son, and all I can really give him is "who I am.". He's helping me to remember spontaneity and honesty, and most importantly, to stop and look around. This is why we are going to spend a year traveling. Here in Marin County not only does one have to keep busy to make ends meet, but it's also the ethic to make progress. Sometimes I find it hard to enjoy being a family. Too often, when I'm in the rat race, my family is more something that I have rather than something I am.

I have never thought of my lifestyle as nontraditional. All except one of my siblings are married, but it seems to make no difference as to the quality of relationship. For me, having a child forms a bond much stronger than a certificate. This is not to say that at some future time we mightn't celebrate our marriage with a ceremony.

Paul Korhummel

What makes my family unique is that I am 24 and I have a brother who is 10 and a brother who is three. The older, Evan, is my father and stepmother's son and the youngest, Bunky, is my mom and Paul's son.. I think that it is wonderful having younger brothers. I got the best of both worlds. I got to experience being an only child for 13 years, and then I got to experience being an older sister. It's been a lot of fun. I feel that I am close to both of my brothers and spend a lot of time with them. I feel very much a part of their lives.

Another thing that is unique about my family is that even though my parents are divorced, we are still all a happy family. Because my parents separated when I was so young, I never really remember them being together and therefore didn't go through the trauma that a lot of older kids do when their parents split up. I still felt very loved and both of my parents were very much involved in my growing up. I hear all the time of people whose parents are divorced and there is nothing but anger and unhappiness, but I never experienced this; we have nothing but love and understanding. We are all a part of each other's lives, and my dad's family even treats my mom, Paul, and Bunky just like any other part of the family, and this makes me very happy.

With all the things going on in the world today, I feel very lucky to have such a wonderful family that gives me so much love and support. Little things, like my mom and dad being divorced or my mom and Paul not being married, don't matter. The only thing that matters is that we are all happy.

Noele Guthrie

Melanie Stone, 45, Paul Korhummel, 42, their son, Nikolai Korhummelstone, 3, and Melanie's daughter, Noele Guthrie, 24. (1991)

In 1976 Eugenie (Genie) and Geoffrey (Jeff) Shields moved from Washington, D.C., back to their childhood neighborhood in Illinois in order to be near both of their families. Jeff's parents live two doors away. Genie's parents, who both died in 1990, also lived nearby. Genie is an art historian, presently working as a teacher part time and developing a cultural history program for elementary-school students. Geoffrey is a lawyer, and Comfort is a college freshman. Janice is a homemaker, and John is a retired investment banker.

Jeff and I grew up in Lake Forest and Lake Bluff, suburbs next to each other north of Chicago. We both have good memories of our childhoods. I had three brothers; Jeff had two sisters and a brother. I lived in a rambling house with a big yard on a ravine. When I was 7, my brothers and I gave my mother a burro for Mother's Day. For the next four years, most Saturdays my father would saddle up the burro and take the four of us on "adventure walks," which usually ended in a pear orchard across town. There were backyard touch football or baseball games, an underground clubhouse in the ravine, sledding down the bluff at the beach, picnics with friends and neighbors. Twice we had people live with us from Latin America for extended periods of time. Especially in the summer, we made frequent trips to Chicago to visit museums and zoos. It was a sheltered and safe existence, partly because it was Lake Bluff, partly because it was the 1950s.

I met Jeff when I was in the seventh grade and our school basketball team played Jeff's Lake Forest team. Jeff and I went to the same high school; we were in the same class. It's interesting to me that both sets of parents had similar experiences. Jeff's parents grew up together in Duluth and were in the same grade in school. My parents grew up together in Highland Park, Illinois. My mother's older brother and my father were friends in school.

Early in our marriage, Jeff and I lived in Vermont. Our life there was idyllic—long walks by the pond to watch the turtles sunning, cross-country skiing in the winter, interesting friends. We always thought we would settle there; it offered the kind of life we felt we wanted after childhoods spent in affluent suburbia. Then our daughter Comfort was born, and shortly after we moved to Washington, D.C. In Washington our son, Jordan, was born. Then began the debate. Where would we move when we finished our work in the senate? After going back and forth for several months, we decided to return to the place where we had grown up, the place where we both had said we would never return. In the end, one fact determined our decision: we wanted to live near our extended families; we wanted our chil-

Eugenie, 45, and Geoffrey B.
Shields, 45, their daughter,
Comfort, 17, their son,
Jordan, 15, and Geoffrey's
parents, Janice, 70, and John
Shields, 70. (1990)

"Our priority was family; it took precedence over jobs, locations, lifestyles. I have never regretted the choice."

— *Eugenie Shields*

dren to spend their early years surrounded by grandparents, aunts, uncles, and cousins. Our priority was family; it took precedence over jobs, locations, lifestyles. I have never regretted the choice.

Some of our friends were incredulous. Why would anyone move to a place for the sole reason of being near their families? How was it possible that we would choose to buy a house just three doors away from in-laws? How could we adjust to Lake Forest after thinking for so long that we would live in Vermont?

It has taken me some time to adjust, but the rest of it has been easy. For this, I thank my parents and especially my parents-in-law. So many of my friends have "in-law" troubles and feel that short, once-yearly visits are infinitely preferable to living down the street. The fact that I don't feel this way is due in large part to the fact that Jeff's parents have always, always made us feel completely welcome in their home. We arrive, and, no matter what they are doing, they sit down with us at the kitchen table and make us feel that whatever we have to say is the most important thing in the world. On the other hand, they almost never drop in on us unannounced. This might seem trivial, but it isn't. It carries the message that their love for us is unconditional, but they also respect our privacy. The other extraordinary thing about them is that they never make judgments or offer advice if we don't ask first. There would be more happy extended families in this country if they followed my in-laws' model.

Although living near our families has been a positive experience, adjusting to Lake Forest has been more difficult for me. I don't like the stereotypical values of Lake Forest any more than when we first arrived here, but little by little I have begun to realize that the community is much more diverse than I originally thought. I don't think the community has changed; my participation has. The more involved I am, the more people I meet who don't fall into materialistic, boring, shallow categories. We have worked to offset the negative effect the community might have on our children: there have been summers on a working farm in Wisconsin, two summers living in a tent and working on an Indian reservation in Wyoming, one summer living in Guatemala. We wanted our children to have experiences beyond the sheltered—and pampered—life in Lake Forest.

The past year has been especially difficult for us. My parents died within eight days of one another. Only a few weeks later, Jordan was diagnosed with juvenile diabetes. Two weeks after his diagnosis, Comfort called from Oxford University to say that she had been in a serious bus accident in which her special friend had died. Comfort has suffered post-traumatic stress; Jordan has had to adjust to a life of daily shots, blood tests, and special diet. We have had to deal with these problems in addition to the pain of the loss of my parents. Looking back on the year, there are long periods I can barely remember. Worse still, during the periods I can remember, I know I was barely functioning. It has been comforting to have extended family near. My brother and Jeff's parents and siblings have all been supportive. I was grateful to be able to be with my parents through their illnesses and their deaths. I am grateful that we are surrounded by our families as we slowly recover.

Eugenie Shields

Once a summer for a three-day weekend, my parents, their four children, each child's spouse, and the nine grandchildren take a "mystery trip." Always within a few hours drive of Chicago, a new location is alternately selected by one of the five nuclear families. Its location is not divulged to the rest of us until the day of the trip, or sometimes through a written puzzle.

Last summer my brother and his wife selected a storytelling convention in rural Woodstock. Other years we have visited wildlife sanctuaries, state parks, downtown Chicago. We have been doing this for a dozen years now.

While we all get together on other occasions—Thanksgiving, Christmas Eve, certain birthdays—the "family weekend" permits depth of visiting through skits, games, chats, and shared experiences. I look forward to this annual event as a measuring of change—especially evident in the children, but quite evident, too, in my peers and parents—an annual passage, like the feet and inches we used to mark on the wall as the kids got older.

Geoffrey B. Shields

Last summer I was studying in Oxford, England. About halfway through the summer program, my group of about sixty students was riding on a double-decker bus to see an art fair. On our way to the fair our bus driver took the turn for the exit off the highway much too fast and our bus turned over. Two people were killed; one was a very close friend of mine. When I called my parents to tell them that my friend Autumn had died, they immediately flew to Oxford to be with me. My parents only stayed for a couple of days because I needed to deal with my friend's death on my own. However, their coming meant a lot to me. They did everything they could to help me.

Since I've been home, my parents have been wonderfully supportive. Almost a year later, I still go through hard times when I have nightmares about the accident or dying or have hallucinations of my friend. I have gone to my mom to talk since I was little. I still go to her to talk about the bus accident. My mom is a special friend. I can trust her with anything. I don't talk to my dad as much or as openly as I do to my mom, but we are just as close. I was having a particularly difficult time a couple of months ago. My dad knew how much it helped me to talk to my friends from Oxford about Autumn's death. He gave me two plane tickets so that two of my Oxford friends could stay with me for a weekend. I was grateful to have the plane tickets, but most of all I was touched that he came up with such a thoughtful idea.

Dealing with Autumn's death has been hard. I don't know how I could have made it without my family. Although my parents don't always understand how

"Although my parents don't always understand how I'm feeling, they unselfishly and magically give freely of themselves and are always ready to listen."

— *Comfort Shields*

I'm feeling, they unselfishly and magically give freely of themselves and are always ready to listen. Instead of breaking us apart, I think that the tragedy of my friend's death has brought my family closer together. It has reminded each one of us how special and precious our love for one another is.

Comfort Shields

I was 15 when my grandparents, my mother's parents, died. Their death was hard for me to understand and accept. I was old enough to appreciate and love them, but I was too young to really know them.

My first memories of my grandparents are still vivid in my mind. My sister and I used to go over to their house and play. Granny would make us "black cow" milkshakes while Poppop gave us underdogs on the swing and tours of the ravine. I'll never forget how Poppop taught me how to make my first paper airplane. These days taught me to love my grandparents.

My grandfather was paralyzed from the waist down when I was in third grade. Granny fell asleep at the wheel while they were on a trip, and the car turned over and ended up in a ditch. I started to appreciate my grandfather as I spent time with him at the hospital and read with him on our living room couch. At ten, I didn't understand his strength. Even though he was paralyzed, Poppop learned to walk with braces. Maybe his determination came from his fighting in World War II; he was a scout who patrolled across enemy lines. He was strong.

Granny died first. I can't remember how I found out or where I was, but I remember her funeral. Actually, it wasn't a funeral at all; it was a party. Granny made it clear that she wanted a party—not a funeral, a party. So that's what she got. Mom brought Dixieland jazz, and there were balloons, and there was Granny. That's when her death hit me.

Poppop died a week later. I was in bed when the phone rang. I answered it. They wanted Mom to go to the hospital. The next morning Mom woke me up, and I knew that Poppop was dead. I don't remember what the medical reason was for his death. We all knew that it was a broken heart. Poppop had been losing ground since the accident, but he held on until Granny died. He loved her.

My sister and I wrote a remembrance for Poppop's memorial service. It wasn't a poem, but it came out a lot like the poem for Granny. I wish I could have had more time with them.

Jordan Shields

My family is what I am about, who I am.

From the time I was 2 years old, following my mother's divorce, she and I lived with her parents in the Minnesota home where she and her brother and sister had grown up. I felt beloved by all. At age 23 I married the girl next door, with whom I'd been in love, off and on, since sixth grade and whom I'd met at birth. (That final statement, too, is no doubt literally true. We were born three days apart in the same hospital to mothers who were friends.) After World War II travels, Jan and I and our first baby, Jeff, came to the Chicago area. Thirty-eight years ago, with a fair amount of trepidation, we signed the mortgage to buy our present house.

We've now been married forty-seven years, a period which has by no means been without negative incident but which, with our work and God's grace, has been predominantly happy. We have four children, all married with what seems to be the same quality and acknowledged source of happiness as ours. Three of those nuclear families have settled in the Chicago area and the fourth, 150 miles away in Champaign. Our grandchildren know us and each other well.

As far back as my memory goes, I've asked God to help me in my family role as it has expanded: please, God, help me to be a good son, a good husband, a good father; and also, a good grandfather. My selfishness sometimes interferes with the response to that daily supplication, sometimes gravely. Nonetheless, that prayer remains my most fervent, and I feel I'm slowly learning how to keep out of the way as God answers it.

I will never have a sibling, but I know as I look at the world about me that its troubles will cease only when I add to my prayer, and am joined by all the other children of the Creator, "Please, God, help me to be a good brother."

John W. Shields

John and I have spent most of our seventy years as husband and wife and best friends. We were born in the same hospital three days apart. That was the beginning of a long adventure together. Through the grades, high school, and college we endured and were married forty-seven years ago.

Our four children, two boys and two girls, grew up in the "hide and seek" Victorian house in which we still live. These great young people have brought four additional special children—their spouses—to our family fold. They're nearby now with our eight grandchildren, enriching each day. They all share their fascinating lives with us.

Widowed when her children were very young, my mother put aside her sadness and made learning fun and loving imperative in our household. The family circle reached out to relatives, friends, and beyond. Her influence helped *us* set *our* goals.

Though no life is real without trauma and anxiety, at 70 years of age I treasure all those years. They've been filled with exciting holidays, family weekends, joyous gatherings around the kitchen table—and so much love.

Grace has been showered on me!
I drew the lucky ticket!
I won at Lotto!
I'm surrounded by 17 blessed people!
Family is what it's all about!

Janice C. Shields

At the time the first photograph was made, Gael Newman had been divorced for eight years and shared custody of Julie with her father, who lived 3,000 miles away. Julie lived with her mother during the school year and with her father and his new family during the summers. Gael married John Pardi, 47, in 1984, four years after the first photograph, and their daughter Kate was born in 1986. The Pardis' home includes rooms for Julie and Kate and for John's two children from a previous marriage, Heather, 21, and Daniel, 17, who visit on weekends. Gael is president and owner of an advertising agency, and John is president and partner in an electronics distribution firm.

I married Julie's dad in 1969 for some vague yet compelling reason that that was what I was supposed to do. I was 20 years old. We moved through the next three years trying to define ourselves and our young little family, mimicking the ways of our parents. Our moms were good, cozy, nurturing moms. So was I. Our moms were good cooks, entertained beautifully, and totally supported their husbands' efforts to provide for their families. And I tried to do the same, yet I was becoming more lost, more depressed. In July of 1972 we separated. It clearly was time for me to find me.

Julie and I lived in Manhattan, and for a short time, Salt Lake City, Utah. In 1978 we moved to a sunny apartment in Berkeley, California. Shortly thereafter the first photo was taken. The challenge for me at that time was to try to find a career that I would enjoy as much as motherhood. Well, nothing is as good as motherhood, but I did find something equally as challenging. In 1980 I started my own advertising agency. Julie was almost 10 years old, and she supported my every effort so endearingly—how could we not make a success of this!

Just before Christmas of 1982, John and I met. He warmed my heart almost instantly, and we married two years later. Julie and I moved from our one-bedroom apartment to a five-bedroom house. Even though John's two children lived with their mother in Marin, we wanted all the children to feel this was their home with their own bedrooms. Julie started high school, and a short time later I became pregnant with Kate. Both John's business and mine were growing rapidly.

Now, John's oldest child, Heather, is a senior in college. Julie is a junior, Daniel is a sophomore in high school, and Kate is in nursery school. As the older children have been sprouting wings (or should I say

wheels!), Kate has been mastering Play-Doh, scissors and glue, and separating from Mom at nursery school. We celebrated the tenth anniversary of my company in October 1990. It has increased in scope from the dining table of our Berkeley apartment to an office suite overlooking a beautiful lake where I work with a half-dozen wonderful people.

John and I contribute equally financially, but that doesn't mean we equally share household routines and obligations. In other words, I take Kate to and from nursery school every day and, more often than not, do the weekly errands to the supermarket, dry cleaners, etcetera, etcetera. The constancy of these responsibilities, coupled with my business, leaves me exhausted. John and I are working on that. I like all that I do at home and in business, but, very simply, it is just too much, leaving little time for me. The hard thing about being a "working mom" (one of our society's weirder expressions), is that no matter where I am or what I'm doing, I feel a pull, a tug, to be taking care of family-business, business-family. All things considered, this is not a tragedy.

My life is great and I am grateful. As time moves along, taking us with it, I hope that I will be able to experience the luxury of being absorbed in whatever I might be doing. No pulls, no tugs, no interruptions...or will that just be boring?

Gael Newman

At the time my career and finances were on a good track, my first family fell apart. My daughter was 8 and my son 4 when I was asked to leave my home and family. My journey through emptiness, guilt, and fear of loneliness was a long and difficult one. With the help and love of friends and professionals, I regained, or found for the first time, a positive sense of my independent self.

I experienced several relationships that were rebound-motivated. As I healed slowly, I was better able to discern motivations, values, emotions, and feelings. As my sense of self-worth has grown, I've been able to enjoy my relationships and better appreciate my life on a day-to-day basis.

Gael and I have been married since 1984. Our daughter Kate is a bright, fun-loving 5-year-old whom I enjoy every day. I'm very fortunate to have a bright, successful, independent wife whose sense of values and family priority, coupled with a generous, loving, and principled approach to life, has helped to keep me on track to a more meaningful and enriched life. My love of work and tendency to mortgage today's happiness for future goals has created challenges and disappointments. Gael's patience and determination have been invaluable in my evolution to a more aware and involved person.

Today my relationship with my first two children is alive and well. My oldest daughter, who is graduating from college, will be living with us until her career is established. Thank God and my wife for this blessing. My son is doing well scholastically and in sports. His mom has done a fine job in raising both these children. I'm appreciative of the nonadversarial environment my children have grown up in with regard to an attitude toward me as a person and as their father. I've missed them every day, but I feel like I do have a family and am able to love and be loved.

Through all that suffering and darkness, I now have a beautiful family of my first two children, my daughter Kate, and a beautiful stepdaughter, Julie.

Who says dreams can't come true?

John Pardi

I am very happy with my life the way it was and the way it is today. Everyone expects that it would have been weird. Everyone asks what it was like to live on two coasts. I have been asked that for God knows how many years — and college interviewers loved to ask it, too. Well, to tell you the truth, it was my life. I loved it, and there wasn't anything especially hard about it for me to deal with. But I've only lived *this* way, so maybe if I had come from a different background, it would be weird, but it isn't. There are the conflicts and the problems, as well as the funny and touching moments that occur, but it's nothing extraordinary — it's my family.

As for my family, Katie is just the most amazing 5-year-old bundle of life. Her personality is just incredible. She's kind of stubborn sometimes about things, but she's always making us laugh. She's an actress and a dancer, and has the cutest little dancer's body that you'll ever see. My stepfather, John, is a wonderful man. As long as he makes Mom happy, he makes me happy. But if he ticks Mom off, he ticks me off too. My one complaint about him is that he chews too loud sometimes, but besides that he is great. He is very helpful to me. My stepsister, Heather, and stepbrother, Dan, are great, too. We always have fun when they visit. My East Coast family, which includes my dad, stepmother, Lois, and their children Anna, Anton, and John are great, too. I enjoy the time I get to spend with them now that I'm on the East Coast. My only frustration is that I have so little time and such a big family. It's hard to break up vacations fairly.

Life is exhilarating but scary these days. I'm living in New Hampshire this summer, just me and my best friend in our very own house! I'm looking forward to graduating next year, but I still want to stay in college forever. Real life looks a lot harder to me now than I thought. I'll adjust just like everyone else does and actually I'm looking forward to the challenge. After school is finished, I want to move to Connecticut and live on a street with big trees, just like Forest Avenue in Berkeley where I grew up. I'm planning on being a second grade teacher. I have a sneaking suspicion Mom will get a house in Connecticut too someday, so we can be close to each other. It's kind of like the *Runaway Bunny* book, where the little bunny runs away and the mother bunny is always right behind him. I wouldn't mind a bit if she did get a house by me as long as my independence was assured. And I know she would let me be independent too.

Julie Christiansen

Gael Newman, 31, and her daughter, Julie Christiansen, 9 years old. (1980)

Gael Newman Pardi, 41, John Pardi, 47, their daughter, Kate, 4, and Gael's daughter, Julie Christiansen, 19. (1990)

Maria Winston and Bob Hoffman were married ten years before they conceived Lucy by in-vitro fertilization. After Lucy was born, they didn't think they wanted more children; however, they are now considering in-vitro fertilization to conceive a second child. Maria and Bob lost their home and all their belongings in the 1991 fire storm that devastated thousands of homes in the Oakland-Berkeley hills in Northern California. This trauma, along with other personal reasons, has influenced them to try to have another child. Maria is a writer, and Bob is an advertising executive; they share family responsibilities.

We conceived Lucy through in-vitro fertilization after seven years of physician-assisted effort. When my pregnancy was confirmed at seven weeks—the tiny heart beating away on the ultrasound screen—our doctor cried, and then told me that I wouldn't need to see specialists anymore; I could go back to my regular obstetrician. After all that time spent being "special," I was wonderfully relieved to be just an ordinary pregnant woman. At 38 years old, I finally became a mother.

Today, I don't much like to talk about infertility, except with women who are going through it. Otherwise, I don't like to talk about the surgeries, the disappointments. I can so easily recall the terrible sadness. At my lowest point, I genuinely felt that my life would be empty without a family. Nothing could make up for that lack: not work, art, friendship, charity, travel, or romance. All those things just seemed like fancy ways to pass the time. The possibility, really the likelihood, of childlessness was so bleak that I could barely look at it.

But that didn't happen. We had Lucy instead. So here we are now, just an ordinary family. And how extraordinary that is! We feel so proud when we walk down the sidewalk pushing our stroller. We enjoy complaining about the ordinary things: Cheerios all over the floor, drool on the shoulders of all our shirts. We know it's not complaining but a kind of disguised rejoicing.

When infertile women ask me about my experience with in-vitro fertilization, I encourage them to try until they can't try any longer. Then when it's over, and their grieving is over, and if they still want a baby, I encourage them to go find one! There are plenty of beautiful children out there; they all deserve a mother's love. And every woman deserves the opportunity, if she wants it, to give that love.

Maria Winston

Yesterday was Father's Day, my first one as a father. I had a free pass to spend it any way I chose. I thought I'd get up early and play some golf.

At 6 a.m. Maria brought Lucy into our bedroom with my Father's Day gift, a sleeve of golf balls with the word "Dad" printed on them. I placed the balls in a drawer and went out to get us some fresh breakfast rolls. I'll play golf some other time, and I'll use some other golf balls.

Bob Hoffman

(Postscript, January 1992)

In October 1991, the house where Helen Nestor photographed us burned down in the catastrophic Oakland-Berkeley fire storm, and we lost all of our possessions. Then, in December, our cousin died suddenly. He was only 44 and left behind a wife and three children. These two events have changed our lives. We don't miss the lost furniture, rugs, paintings. We do miss all of the photographs. And we miss our cousin Joel.

Before the fire we had decided not to have any more children. I'm 40 now, Bob's 46, and with Lucy at eighteen months, our routine is stable and predictable. But the desire rose up in me to have another child. Slowly, over a period of months, it became clear to me that I just have to try. Look at Lucy: what if we can make another one this wonderful? So we've decided to try. Maybe in-vitro fertilization will work again and we'll have another little life to love.

Maria Winston

Maria Winston, 39, and Bob Hoffman, 45, and their daughter, Lucy, ten months old. (1991)

Joanna and James Harris were married seven years when they adopted Jennifer. Two years later they adopted Jonathon, a Vietnamese orphan. James is a veterinarian and Joanna, at that time, was working as director of creative arts therapy at a local college. They separated three years after the first photograph was made. Joanna has physical custody of the children and they share legal custody, with Jennifer and Jonathon spending every other weekend with their father as well as once a week dinners and some vacation time. Joanna and the children were photographed again in 1989.

We are now a single-parent family. The children have lived with me since 1980, and I have raised them, *alone*. Jennifer and Jonathon were adopted, Jenny from Children's Home Society and Jonathon from Catholic Relief, at the end of the Vietnam war. Our family is interracial.

I grew up in a traditional orthodox Jewish urban family with strong European cultural biases and standards. Responsibility for the children's health, education, recreation, and daily care is very difficult with limited funds and energy. Men simply abandon the family.

I do the best I can to make a good life for them—and still have some energy left for my life. I hope my children have chances to learn, to travel, to work, to love and be loved as they deserve. I would change the lousy divorce laws of California and be more selfish and assertive on behalf of my children. I would have done more for *myself* during marriage so I had more resources now.

Socially, we are generally outcast by the larger community. In England, I was asked if I were an "embassy nanny." Only a few close friends accept and enjoy our unique family.

Joanna Harris

Changing times is an understatement! My first marriage with two biological children ended in divorce some fourteen years prior to the photograph of my second family taken in 1977. My first two children, now aged 32 and 30, are very close to me, and we have regular contact, in spite of their mother's negative influence during their adolescence and my second wife's hostility towards them.

I was married twelve years before the photograph of my second "family" was taken. At first I was reluctant to have children. As time progressed, my feelings changed. I was an only child, a depression baby. Times were tough. I wanted more children. I wanted to parent children throughout their childhood and adolescence. I also believed that children would help to stabilize my somewhat rocky second marriage. We tried to "make children." It did not work, which in itself was traumatic, so we "bought two." Kids are kids, biological or adopted it's the same, except with adopted ones you don't have the genetic expectations. It's a surprise! I felt like a miniature United Nations and still do. I like the feeling.

Three years after the 1977 photo the marriage failed, and we separated. A very bitter time ensued. I was determined to keep contact with these children and not let the "war" interfere. I had no idea how hard it would be. They are now, fourteen years later, independent, self-sufficient children.

History does repeat itself. My second wife worked very hard to handicap me as the noncustodial parent, but I persevered! The children do call and confide in me. The court system does not help, and neither does the available social service system. You have to do it yourself. It's tough. Nothing worthwhile comes easy, and there are no instant rewards.

I guess the family as an institution is not a bad one. I am married again to a woman I have lived with for eight years. My two oldest children call her "Mom," sort of humorous, since she is only six years older than my eldest son. Some day perhaps the younger children will call her "Mom," too. They do confide in her. As for more children, we have three dogs, five cats, and seventy birds, and breed and raise macaws and rare Amazon parrots and fish.

Would I do it again? Hell, yes!

James M. Harris

What is unique is that we are all so racially different. What is best is that we all love and care for each other very much. I wish that we wouldn't stand out so much in public places just because we are different.

Jennifer Harris

We all come from different parts of the world. We care for each other and go on trips together and do things together. I wish we could get about one billion dollars and we also wouldn't have to pay taxes.

Jonathon Harris

Joanna, 43, and, James
Michael Harris, 43, and their
children, Jennifer, 4, and
Jonathon, 2 years old.
(1977)

Joanna Harris and her children, Jennifer, 16, and Jonathon, 14. (1989)

Fred and Jennifer Aono grew up in the Midwest and consider themselves to be a typical Midwestern family. Two years after they were married, they had their first child Marissa. The Aonos wanted more children but suffered two miscarriages, each in the second trimester, with the second miscarriage involving twins. Later, they had their daughter Alexandra and are now considering having more children, although they are concerned about possible miscarriages. Jennifer's parents were sent to an internment camp for Japanese-Americans during World War II, and although her parents do not speak of this often, Jennifer knows this was a painful part of her family's history. Jennifer works part time as an elementary school teacher, and Fred is an immunobiologist.

I have four sisters, and they are all younger than me. While growing up I was treated quite well because I was the oldest and was therefor looked up to as the wisest. I don't think this has anything to do with our being Japanese but just that our family is this way. I was closest to the oldest sister when I was younger, but now that we have all grown up I've become closest to the youngest sister.

My dad treats me in a way that is very Japanese. He really doesn't show emotion toward me because I'm a male, which is very traditional Japanese. I can't ever remember him hugging me. There are pictures of me sitting on his lap, but I don't have any memories of him being overtly affectionate with me. It's a different story with my sisters. He is always hugging them and kissing them. There are different ways my dad shows me that he loves me. It's okay that he doesn't hug me. It's hard to explain, but I can tell he cares for me, like when he directs the conversation toward me. I know that he's very interested in what I'm doing and in what I think—that's his way of showing me affection. That's the way his father treated him, and, like me, he was the only boy in his family. My wife and I don't have a son, but if we did, I'd be hugging him and would show affection toward him. Part of the reason I would do it differently is because of my separation from the traditional Japanese culture and because of the importance of being physically affectionate with children. I would feel restrained if I couldn't show affection to my children. It would be an effort not to hug them.

I was born in Chicago, but my family moved around a lot when I was a child. I lived in totally white neighborhoods, and there were no Japanese or Oriental people in the area. I never really noticed any racism when I was growing up. If anything, my being Japanese was considered a novelty that was helpful to me. I felt that the reason I was popular was because I was a minority, but it's hard to say if I would have been popular if I wasn't a Japanese-American. My dad traveled a lot when I was younger and my mother took care of the family at home. When I was 3 I had a 1-year-old sister, and then my Mom had twins. There were five children all together. We lived in a three-story flat and my aunt lived on the third floor with my grandma and grandpa. They used to take us a lot of places. I was very close to my grandparents and aunt.

My parents have lived in the same city for twenty-three years, and I live only a few blocks away. So my

Fred, 33, and Jennifer Aono, 35, and their daughters, Marissa, 6, and Alexandra, 2. (1990)

children are growing up in the same neighborhood that I grew up in. The main difference between then and now is that when I was growing up there were are quite a few. As a parent, I feel I am involved with the my family's daily activities, although Jenny is with them more because she only works half a day as a teacher. When I was growing up, my parents were only slightly involved in the kids' social and school activities. Jenny and I have been involved in our own children's school activities because we feel it's important.

My parents stressed education when I was growing up, and we do the same. When I was young, there were a lot of kids my age who considered college an option—for me it was thought of as a requirement. Education was valued in my family, and I looked forward to going to college. I would be shocked to hear my children say they didn't want to go to college. We have already started their college accounts!

Jenny and I had our first child, Marissa, two years after we were married. Jenny then had a miscarriage before we had our second daughter, Alexandra. After Alex, Jenny miscarried again. As the father, it was devastating going through this. For me, the hardest part was that Jenny was hurting so bad. Anybody who has gone through this experience knows that it's hard to know what to say. It was also hard to know when Jenny needed to talk about it and when she didn't. Emotions ebb and flow. People don't realize that any little thing can be a reminder of the loss. The miscarriages made me understand that Jenny was bound to the baby as soon as she knew she was pregnant. I realized how much she really wanted each child. We would like to have more children now that we have our two daughters, but my only fear is of what Jenny has to go through. Today we are extremely happy, and those painful experiences remind us of how happy we really are.

My parents taught me to value family, and now I am passing that on to my own. Family is the single most important thing. You could say we are a typical Midwestern family. We are not affiliated with any church or religion, but, other than that, we're pretty typical. Our family is the primary focus of everything that I do. Every decision made takes the well-being of our family into consideration. These decisions include career, social activities, budget, free time, education, religion, and health to name a few. Our immediate family is the ultimate source of strength in hard times. It is also without a doubt the source of the most numerous and greatest joys. These are usually manifested as "simple pleasures" such as silly times together, first words, and embarrassing moments. It is inconceivable for me to picture a life without my wife and daughters.

Fred Aono

I grew up as an only child in a very close-knit family in Chicago. Sometimes this was lonely, although I had a couple of cousins I played with. My parents are second-generation Japanese-Americans, but the neighborhood I grew up in was primarily Caucasian. My parents were both sent to internment/concentration camps during World War II, but they don't talk about it much. My mother seems very bitter about the camp, about being interned and the way they were treated. One experience she told me about that sticks in my mind is how the best meat was taken by certain people in charge, leaving the internees hardly anything at all. My father was an ambulance driver in the camp. He doesn't seem as bitter about the internment as my mother. I just couldn't imagine leaving all of my worldly possessions (even a pet) behind or selling them for practically nothing to live behind barbed wire. Could you?

I consider my own family traditional in the sense that we do things and live pretty much the same as all the other suburban families around us. My husband and I both work, and Grandma takes care of my younger daughter, Alex. My children participate in different activities—piano, tennis, preschool, gymnastics. My 8-year-old, Marissa, and her class are participating in a "special buddy" program at school where each child works with another child from the special education class. Her school has participated in lessons about different countries, and there are children from different countries in her class. Marissa is beginning to realize that there are differences between people. Up until now race has not been an issue with my daughter because she really wasn't aware of it. Occasionally, she has been made fun of by other children who taunt her by talking gibberish as if imitating a native Asian. It's unfortunate that I have to explain why these things happen. Racism is a concern of mine. In many ways I feel it more as an adult than I did as a child. Now, as an adult, if there's an altercation, for example as a driver, the fact that I'm Japanese, as well as a woman, always comes up right away.

I want my children to learn that they can accomplish and be anything they want to be. I want them to believe in themselves and not let other people's opinions interfere or influence their lives. I was taught that if I believe in something that I should stick to my convictions. The hardest part for me as a parent is trying not to interfere in my children's lives too much. I have to teach them to stick up for themselves and that I should not get involved. Children don't take things as personally as adults; they can be enemies one day and best friends the next. Their feelings are hurt, and the next minute they forget about it. It's hard to see my children's feelings hurt and not get involved. I'm sure that in a few more years the hardest part of parenting will be dealing with other issues.

A happy and secure family life provides a nurturing environment that all members need in order to develop as individuals. We all share with each other, and we all learn from each other. My family is my priority; they are my best friends, and they are the most important part of my life. One major hurt is that I have had two miscarriages in the second trimesters of the pregnancies. The second pregnancy was twins. This memory will never leave. I will always remember my lost babies. I would like to have four or five children, and I'm thinking of getting pregnant again, but I'm scared. I am grateful for the two healthy children I do have.

Everything and anything about my family brings me joy. Spending time with them, even if it's just doing the simplest things, is wonderful. It's always something different with the kids and just the simplest expression or phrase can make it a memorable experience.

Jennifer Aono

I have a family. I really love them. I have four people in my family. First is my sister, Alexandra. She is my best friend. She is 3 years old. She does not go to school. She likes to goof around. She hates to clean. Her favorite color is white. Her favorite number is eight. She can count to twenty. She knows most of her colors. Her favorite animal is an alligator.

Second is my dad. He gets mad sometimes, but I still love him. He likes to scare me and my sister. He likes to go out. Third is my mom. She likes to clean. She hates to go out to eat. She is nice to us. I feel very happy when my family is near. We do a lot of things together. My favorite thing is going to the zoo. I learned that my family is the best thing there is.

Marissa Aono

Linda and Ernie Lorimer married in 1977 and have had a commuting marriage during much of that time. Linda is the president of Randolph-Macon Women's College in Virginia, and Ernie is a partner in a Connecticut law firm. The family lives in Lynchburg, Virginia, and Ernie makes the trip between Virginia and Connecticut weekly. Linda's responsibilities as president involve many official events in which Ernie cannot participate, and in turn, Linda cannot meet Ernie's clients. Nevertheless, they find other ways to support each other's careers and nourish their family life.

We have a traditional sense of family but a nontraditional "schedule" for a family, caused by a commuting marriage. With a mom, dad, two children, a tank of fish, junior choir practice, and soccer games, our family looks and feels remarkably like the ones in which Ernie and I were reared. The difference is that Ernie spends his weekdays in Connecticut practicing law and, for the last five years, has commuted to Virginia on the weekends so that I could follow my heart to serve women's education as president of Randolph-Macon Women's College. Our nontraditional schedule is further complicated by the fact that my work entails frequent travel and long days. It has a public dimension not only for me, but also for Peter, Kelly, and Ernie, who regularly change out of their khakis and play clothes and get dressed up—like in the pictures—to greet alumnae, trustees, and other college visitors.

The week of our son's first birthday, I got the invitation to be president at Randolph-Macon. I thought, "How in the world could we do this?" The college was in Virginia, and Ernie's legal practice would not lend itself to relocating, so I hemmed and hawed for about a week. Ernie, knowing my devotion to women's colleges, said, "Look, very few people get to do something they really believe in. You should just do it, and we will figure out a way to make it happen." We knew full well what was entailed in a commuter marriage, since we had previewed the arrangement a decade before, when, early in our marriage, we had commuted between New York and Connecticut when I was at Yale and Ernie was practicing law on Wall Street. From our days as classmates in law school to our years both working as lawyers in New York to a decade of parenthood, we have a tight fabric of feeling that we cherish and which sustains us through the craziest of our weeks.

A commuting marriage should not be entered into lightly or unadvisedly, for I find the separation to be a real sacrifice. However, it has not been quite as difficult as I expected, for two reasons. The first is that the children seem very settled and happy in Virginia, and we work hard to make them think of this place as their home. The other is that Ernie has only missed a handful of weekends in the last five years so there is a predictability to our schedule, which is a comfort to the children and to me. We all regret not having more time together. When our son Peter said in earnest recently, "Why don't we move the college to Connecticut?" I realized he was saying something for all of us. I am helped by the fact that I am a part of a college that sees itself as a real community. Some afternoons Peter and Kelly come after school to play in

Linda, 39, and Ernest Lorimer, 39, and their children, Kelly, 10, and Peter, 7. (1991)

my office while I am working. They are now old enough to enjoy the rich range of college events. It is wonderful that we can all go together to see a modern dance concert or a varsity basketball game or take a family picnic to the intercollegiate horse show. The lines between work and play, family and profession, are very fuzzy in our case. And at times there are frustrations, but more often there are satisfactions.

When I was growing up, my father was in the Navy, and there were years when he was away for six months at a time. I thought he was the best dad in the world, and I never thought I suffered by his absences. His schedule was just the way he led his life. I hope my children have the same acceptance of my work and their dad's schedule.

Both my parents conveyed to my brother and to me that they thought we could do anything we wanted to. They never made me feel strange for preferring a baseball and bat to a Barbie doll. I hope I am conveying to our children the same sense to find and follow their own interests wherever they may lead. I think today there are many more families who, like us, are trying to define their joint life in ways that derive naturally from their particular circumstances rather than relying on a particular script or structure for what a family is supposed to be or do. It will be interesting to see what we find for our future.

Linda Lorimer

I am baffled when people suggest that our commuting marriage makes us a role model for the modern family. It is not a model to which anyone should aspire; it is simply the best arrangement we could arrive at for the particular set of circumstances and opportunities we find at this stage of our lives. So for the time being, it works—and that's all that matters.

It takes me about five hours to commute from Connecticut to Virginia. I am usually home Saturday and Sunday, and then I return to Connecticut on Monday. We have a little house in Connecticut where I stay during the week, and when I leave for the weekend, I simply travel with a briefcase. I treat the commute like a long subway ride home. I don't think too much about the commute, because from early on in our marriage I was the commuting member of the family. When Linda was working at Yale and I was in New York City, I would spend an hour and twenty minutes each way commuting by train. And for a year and a half, before the family moved to Virginia, I drove an hour each way to work. In some respects, the actual commuting is now easier, since I do it once a week.

When we started this long-distance arrangement, Kelly was 5 and Peter was 1 and a half years old. Our primary concern was the effect of the separation on them, and Linda and I had a clear understanding that we would reunite the family at any point if we perceived or suspected that the commute was having an adverse affect on them or on our marriage. We have been lucky so far.

The kids seem better adjusted than I am to the fact that their dad will not be around for the class play or to help with homework. I wouldn't say I feel guilty about that, but I do feel a couple of pangs. On the other hand, our children have a world that is much more solidly put together and reliable than that of many kids. Many come from broken homes or have financial distress. Our children have a family, well knit together, and they have been physically located in one place for a long period of time. We are economically comfortable, and the kids are doing well in school. Those are all advantages that are becoming highly unusual and perhaps are more unusual than a commuting dad.

I don't think Linda's and my marriage has suffered at all from the commute. We are as tight as we ever were, but we do have significant phone bills. I think we both regret that we cannot do as much as we might for each other's career. I am not around to help host a lot of the events at the President's House; and by the same token, she can't do any of the traditional spousal hosting for me. But we provide a lot of emotional support.

Our children have been the source of our greatest satisfaction. I think we want to pass on to our kids the values we have. We are interested in seeing them creatively challenged so they can sort things out for themselves. In that respect, Peter's saying, "Why don't you move the college to Connecticut?" is a welcome question. It's important to us that they are prepared to think about the way things are and ask us if they can be better.

Ernie Lorimer

To show our family, you really need a photo album. It would show our family's tickling battles, lots of spaghetti and chili dinners, our shirttails untucked, Dad at his computer, all of us sailing on Saturday, car tournaments, and Peter pretending he is a dog, or an airplane, or a Ninja Turtle.

Kelly Lorimer

PHOTO: PAMELA VALOIS

Helen Nestor's love of old family photographs and desire to document the disappearing innocence of her own three children in photographs led her to photography at the age of 35 and becoming a professional photographer. After studying with Morley Baer, Ansel Adams, and Minor White, Nestor turned to documentary work, which ranged from the Free Speech Movement in the early 1960's through desegregation and school busing, the Haight-Ashbury flowerchild era, the beginnings of the contemporary womens' movement, and portraits of midlife women. An attack of polio when Nestor was 27 left her walking with crutches and concern with problems of the disabled. Nestor documented her own hospital experiences, and in 1972 she photographed pilgrims who had gone to Lourdes, France, seeking miracle cures. She has done photographic series on self-defense for disabled women and disabled women working.

Fascinated by the variety of new family arrangements Nestor was witnessing in the late 1970's and the involvement of her own children and friends in nontraditional systems, she decided to explore the multitude of options that were beginning to present themselves. She began to photograph nontraditional families in 1978, a project that would span 14 years and result in *Family Portraits in Changing Times*.

Helen Nestor's photographs and photo essays have been published in books and magazines, and exhibited in museums and galleries in the U.S. and in Europe. She lives with her husband in Berkeley, California.

Judith Stacey is a leading authority on the postmodern family, focusing on gender, family, and social change in the United States. Her recently published book, Brave New Families: Stories of Domestic Upheaval in Late Twentieth-Century America, was a 1991 finalist for the C. Wright Mills Award of the Society for the Study of Social Problems. Stacey is currently a professor of sociology and women's studies at UC Davis where she has taught since 1979. In addition to authoring three books, Stacey's articles are included in nearly 20 books and anthologies internationally.